The "Write" Stuff
How to Produce, Publish and Promote Your Own Book

By:
C. L. Threatt

The "Write" Stuff
How to Produce, Publish and Promote Your Own Book
By:
C. L. Threatt
Copyright © 2016
Layout and cover design by Lisa Benn
Edited by Chianti Cleggett

All rights reserved.
No part of this publication may be reproduced or transmitted in any form or by any means without written permission from the author except for quotations in a review.

Ahava Publishing, LLC
65 Twisted Oak Circle
Odenville, AL 35120
(205) 213-8472
E-mail: CL3tt@windstream.net
Website: www.cedricthreatt.com

Printed in USA

This book is dedicated to those who refuse to give up on their dream.

ACKNOWLEDGMENTS

First of all, I'd like to thank my beautiful wife, Sharmon, there is no me without you. You're the most supportive person I know. Thanks for seeing and sharing my vision and for always being in my corner. To Mrs. Patrick and Mrs. Denson, thanks for seeing the gift in me I never knew I had. Thanks also for your continued encouragement and support. To Lisa Benn, thanks once again for adding your creative talents to my work and making it look so good. To Chianti Cleggett, thanks for correcting my grammar as only you can and helping me grasp the concept of addition by subtraction. To Hasani Pettiford, I know our paths didn't cross by accident. Thanks for mentoring and showing me how to take my talents to another level. To my parents who always taught me that hard work and honesty pays off. To everyone who purchases and reads this book, I say a huge and sincere Thank You. I owe you a great deal of gratitude because I consider every book sale a compliment. I am indeed humbled by your generosity. May God continue to bless you all.

CONTENTS

Introduction ………………………............................6

Section One: How to Produce Your Book ……………9

Chapter One: What to Write and How ..…………………11

Chapter Two: When to Write……………………………..39

Chapter Three: Designing a Cover ..………………….…..47

Section Two: How to Publish Your Book ……………….61

Chapter Four: Traditional Publishing ..………………….63

Chapter Five: Other Choices in Publishing……………....77

Chapter Six: Things Your Book Will Need …………….97

Section Three: How to Promote Your Book ……….107

Chapter Seven: Marketing and Promotion ...……………109

Chapter Eight: The Business of Being an Author …….133

Introduction:

So you want to write a book? Congratulations. You've made the first step in what could be your destiny. Of course wanting to write a book and actually writing it are two different things. Many people want to do something, but never really do it. Obviously you're not one of those people because otherwise you wouldn't have opened this book.

Now that you've decided to write your own book, you've probably asked yourself many questions such as: What should I write? Where do I start? When do I start? How long should it be? Should I pursue a mainstream publisher, or should I self-publish? These and other questions will be addressed in this book.

After more than 10 years of being in the industry, I can tell you through experience that the answers to the questions above depend solely on you. That's the beauty of writing your own book. You get to decide when and how you want to proceed. Some people decide to wait until they've taken a writing course or have had some other type of training before they begin, while others dive right in without getting any training at all.

Regardless of your skill level, writing a book is something that can be simultaneously challenging and frustrating. But, the fun you'll have and the lessons you'll learn in the process will outweigh any challenges or frustrations you may incur. Just think of how good you'll feel after seeing your book completed and how many people will be able to enjoy it. It won't be easy. Like anything else, you'll get out of it what you put into it. It'll take a lot of discipline and determination. But, in the end, it will be well worth it.

Make no mistake, this is not a book that will tell you how to write a book in 30 days and become a multi-millionaire. If that's what you're looking for, you might as well stop reading and put it down now. And, while I won't guarantee you success after reading this book – no one can do that – I hope that after you've gone through these three informative lessons, you will have a better understanding and feel more comfortable about how to produce, publish and promote your very own book. In these pages, I've compiled the things I've learned over the years as well as information from other noted professionals that will help you along your journey of becoming a published author. Please note that the information shared in this book is current as of the time it is written. Like all industries, some of the rules of publishing may change in the future, but there are also some that will always remain the same. So what do you say? Let's get started.

Section 1
How to Produce a Book

Chapter One

What to Write and How

This is how you do it: you sit down at the keyboard and you put one word after another until it's done. It's that easy, and that hard.

— Neil Gaiman

Congratulations! You've decided to write a book. Good luck on your journey. Of course you know it won't happen overnight. It's going to take you a while to get it done. How long it will take is totally up to you. So what do you want write? Do you know? Deciding what to write is just as important and can be just as difficult as deciding how to write it.

Before you start writing your book, I believe there are a few questions you should ask yourself. First, why do you want to write a book? Is it because you love writing or is it because you feel you have something important to say? Are you committed to it? Are you passionate about it? Are you willing to go the extra mile? Secondly, what do you hope to accomplish by writing your book? Do you want to just have a book to share with your family and friends, or do you want to have one to share with the whole world? Do you want to leave a legacy? Do you want to sell a few copies, or do you want to be on the *New York Times* Best Seller list? Regardless of your goals, writing your book will take patience, commitment and a lot of self-confidence and self-discipline. Many will try, some will quit, only a few will succeed. Which one will you be?

Writing a book comes with its own set of challenges. You don't want to make the job harder than it has to be. If you're like me, you want to make it as simple and enjoyable as you possibly can. How do you do that? By first deciding what you want to write and how you plan to write it. Do you want to write fiction or nonfiction? Do you want to write for children or adults? Do you want your writing to be humorous or serious? These are just a few of the questions you'll have to ask yourself before you get started. After you've answered these questions you're ready to begin your journey.

Writing Nonfiction

If you want to write nonfiction, you can start by writing about what you know. And what do you know? Well, I'm sure you know a lot of things. As a matter of fact, you probably know more than you think you do. Think about a subject you know something about, or maybe something that interests you. It can be your vocation, a hobby, a passion of yours, or maybe even an experience you've had. Is there something you'd like to teach people? You can teach what you know, or teach people how to do what you do. Remember, you're the expert. At least that's what people will see you as after you've completed your book, as well, they should. Everybody's an expert at something.

People read books for different reasons. Some will read for information while others read for entertainment. Nonfiction books are read for information – be it a self help, a motivational or even a cook book. Fiction books however, are read for entertainment. Sometimes people like to get away from the hustle and bustle of real life and reading a book is a great way to do it. Fiction books offer a way of escape, that's why, if they're written properly, people can get lost in them. If you'd like to write fiction, whether children's books or novels for adults, you have to have a great imagination. People who write fiction are imaginative, creative and have a great knack for storytelling. So how do you begin to write your book of fiction?

Writing Fiction

Probably the most popular genre of fiction writing is children's books. If you want to write for children, there are a few things you need to consider. First, decide what type of children's book you'd like to write. Will your book have pictures? Will it be a rhyming book or have normal dialogue? Will it have human, animal or some other type of inanimate characters?

Contrary to popular belief, writing for children is not as easy as one might think. It's quite the contrary. Children are smarter than you think and they can be some of the hardest readers to satisfy. Children can be brutally honest when it comes to telling you what they think about your book. Thus, if you want to know whether or not your book is worth presenting to the public, you should test it by reading it to children first (not your own or their friends). Visit a local library, an elementary school, or day care center and try it out. Notice the children's reactions and ask for their opinions. This is a great way to see if you're on the right track.

Picture Books

If you're writing a picture book, keep in mind that the standard length is between 24-32 pages, but there are some exceptions. Some may be shorter or longer, but they must have a page count that's a multiple of eight. That's because all books are printed on what's called signatures and each signature is 16 pages. Picture books are normally shorter than most books so that's why this rule is all the more important. Also, keep in mind that your front matter which includes your title page, copyright page, dedication, etc. and your back matter, which includes your about the author page, order form, acknowledgements, appendix, index, etc. may take up to four or five pages. That means you need to subtract these pages from 32 to come up with the number of pages you'll have for actual content. Also, keep in mind that you probably should limit your word count to no more than 2000 words. Again, there may be exceptions to this rule.

Where to Find Ideas

So where do you find ideas for writing a children's book? Do they come from voices in your head? Or, do they come from everyday normal activities? If you take time to notice, ideas are all around you. They can come from anywhere, be it a personal childhood experience or from watching children at play on a school playground or in a park. Ideas can come from your dreams, or maybe from just remembering people, places or things from your childhood like your siblings, a pet, a favorite toy, or the vacation spot you and your family visited every year. I've gotten ideas from driving down the road and seeing a billboard and even from little sayings I've used around my house or heard other people use. Paying attention to your surroundings and hanging out with children are other great ways to help bolster your creative juices. Also, paying attention to trends and what's popular at the present time in our culture may help. Keep in mind though that just because something is popular today doesn't mean it will be popular by the time your book is released to the public. Visit your local library or bookstore and pay attention to other children's books. Notice their sizes, texture and colors. While you're at it, take time to read some of them as well, because reading children's books by other authors and noticing their style of writing and how they flow can and will give you some idea of how to write your own.

Research

Whether you're writing for children or adults, chances are you'll need to do some research before writing your book. I'm reminded of a conference I attended where other children's authors were in attendance. In one of the breakout sessions, an author/illustrator shared how his uncle, who was a farmer, complimented him on how perfectly he had depicted cows in a field through his pictures. The author/illustrator had drawn a picture of white cows in a field with dirt on their knees. His uncle told him that cows always have dirty knees from being on them all the time in the grass. Talk about paying attention to detail. That's why, whether you're writing or illustrating for children, doing your research is so important. In fact, you may find even more ideas from doing research.

A lot of writers stray away from doing research because they hated doing it for certain projects when they were in school. But think of it this way, this is not research you're doing for a term paper you've been assigned from a teacher or professor. It's quite the contrary. This is something *you're* interested in doing, so it should be fun. This is the same advice I often give to parents of children who don't like to read. I suggest that they have their child read books on subjects that pique their curiosity. That way it's done for fun and doesn't feel so much like a task.

Parents tell me that this has done wonders for their child's interest in reading, and it will do the same for you and your research. After all, if you want to be a great writer, you have to also be willing to be a great reader.

Research is simply gathering, arranging and condensing all the information you've read and taken notes on. When doing research for your book, you should have so much information that it'll be hard to decide what to leave behind. The Internet is a great place to start your research. There you'll find more up-to-date information than a library or bookstore. You can use Google search, a blog or any other online forum to get started. You can also read certain magazine articles and newspapers to gather information. Anytime you find something pertaining to your subject either by reading, watching TV, or hearing an important statistic or quote, write it down and file it in a folder to use later.

Although your audience may be children, keep in mind that your book must appeal to adults as well. After all, they're the parents and they're the ones who will purchase your book, so they need to be sold on it too. No parent wants their child to read anything they don't approve of, nor will they want to spend their hard earned money on it. Therefore, choose your subject matter carefully.

If you're writing a book for young adults, the 32 page count rule doesn't apply because it will probably take more than 32 pages to tell your story. However, I still do not recommend that you make it too long. I think 150-200 pages will suffice. If it turns out where you need more pages, Tracey E. Dils[1], in her book titled, *You Can Write Children's Books*, suggests turning your book into a series, which will give you more books in the future. Of course, this is only a suggestion. The final decision is totally up to you.

How to Create Characters

All stories need characters and all characters need names. They also need a personality and other attributes. So how do you create all of this? There are several ways. One way to create characters is, again, to just pay attention to your surroundings. Watch people and their mannerisms. Your characters can be based on your coworkers, family members, old acquaintances, or a neighbor down the street. Need names for your characters? Make them up, use your pet's name, a street name, or use the names of people you know by combining one person's first name with another person's last name. Never use someone's real name without first getting their permission.

When creating your character(s), keep in mind that there are three types you may need. First, you need a major character. This is the main character in your story (i.e. Dorothy in *The Wizard of Oz*). Your main character can be your protagonist or hero, someone you want your readers to root for. Be sure to make them as realistic as possible with normal quirks, emotions and common flaws. Talk about what makes them happy, sad or angry.

Since you're going to have a main character, then you'll need to have minor characters as well (i.e. Toto, The Scarecrow, The Tin Man and The Cowardly Lion). And, if your main character is going to be a protagonist, that means you'll also need an antagonist (i.e. The Wicked Witch). Like your main character, your antagonist should have their share of realistic human characteristics. Of course, you don't have to limit yourself to only one main character and one antagonist. You can have as many as you'd like, but I would suggest no more than three. Having too many may be confusing to your reader and cause them to lose interest.

When writing your story, determine what you want your main character's goal to be. In *The Wizard of Oz*, Dorothy's goal was to get back home to Kansas. Give your character obstacles to overcome before they reach their goal, each one being more difficult than the one before. Also, grab your reader's attention from the beginning. This is called your hook.

Like any print or broadcast journalist, you need to tell every story by giving your reader the answer to the five W's. The first W is *who*. Tell your reader who your character is in the beginning and don't forget to mention their attributes that I discussed earlier. You can also introduce the conflict your character is facing at the beginning. Secondly, you need to tell *what* your character is trying to accomplish. The third W is *when*. The *when* can be the moment in time your story is set. It can be in the past, the present, or even the future. Choose your words carefully to make your reader feel as if they are really present in the story. Speaking of words, make sure the dialect you give your character fits the time they're in, unless they're in a different time than the other characters. Also, be aware of your vocabulary. Write for the age of your audience. You don't want your words to be too elementary for older kids, or too advanced for younger ones.

The fourth W is *where*. Like the when, the where plays an important part in capturing and holding your readers' attention. This is where you set the scenery for your story. Finally, the fifth W is *why*. Why is your character doing what he or she is doing, and why should your reader care? Including these five W's in your story will go a long way towards your success as a writer. If you leave any of them out, your story will seem incomplete and leave your reader confused.

The Plot

After you've decided how you want to describe the five W's to your reader, it's time to develop a plot. This is where you formulate your sequence of events. In other words, where is your story going? Don't be afraid to add subtle or obvious twists and turns along the way. Your plot can be simple for early readers in a picture book, or a little more complex for older ones such as middle or high school age kids who like to read chapter books. Each chapter can build on the previous one, or you may decide to make each one stand on its own while staying true to the storyline. When writing a chapter book, whether for children or adults, don't get overly concerned with writing each one in sequential order. You can write your last chapter first and write your first one last, if you like. Or, you may want to begin with one that will be placed in the middle of your book and then go back and complete the others. Start by writing the chapter that comes easiest to you first. A good practice is to keep folders and label them with the title of your chapters and place notes in them accordingly whenever a thought or an idea comes to mind.

Before you start writing your book, it's a good idea to find other books pertaining to the subject you want to write about. Go to Amazon.com or other online bookstores and see how many you can find (5 or 6 should suffice). Read and analyze them. Consider what you would add to them or say differently? If you don't want to purchase the books, borrow them from the library. This may seem like a lot of reading, but trust me, you'll enjoy it. It'll give you a chance to see how other authors write and how they make their words flow. Collect notes or create a word document to organize your information. Make the file name the same as the title of your book. You can also collect your notes in a three-ring binder and place separators in it for each chapter. Always keep a pen and paper handy so wherever you are if a new thought hits you, you can jot it down until you get home and then place the information in the appropriate chapter in your binder.

You may decide to include a subplot. This is a great way to introduce your minor characters who have their own set of characteristics like the ones I discussed earlier. For example, notice how the minor characters in *The Wizard of Oz* were introduced to the story. Also notice how each one of them came with their own problem and how it correlated with the main one in the story.

Your minor characters should interact with your main character but never overshadow him or her. Subplots help keep your story moving and give it added interest. When determining your plot and subplot, ask yourself *what if this or that happened* type questions to decide what comes next. Try to always keep your reader guessing. Again, this is where your imagination and creativity should shine.

Dialogue

Dialogue is one way to define your characters. It's what helps move the story along. Make sure your reader knows who's speaking and when. Avoid using fancy words like *retorted* when a simple *he said* or *she said* will do. This is more natural. To eliminate confusion of who's speaking, start a new paragraph whenever a different person is speaking or when someone new enters the conversation. After a while, you won't have to use *he said* or *she said* at all because your reader will be able to tell who's speaking by the natural flow of your words. Sometimes you may want to use adjectives like *she said happily*, but make sure not to overuse them. If a character is speaking to himself or herself, be sure to italicize their words (i.e. Tony thought to himself *I've got to find a way out of here.*). Also, try not to make your sentences too long. Stay true to your character's dialect, slang and grammar. Make sure it fits their personality.

Writing a Novel

If you've decided to write a novel, the same rules I mentioned earlier such as character description, having a hook, creating conflict, dialogue and telling the five W's still apply, in some cases even more so. American science fiction author Nancy Ann Dibble said, "Make everybody fall out of the plane first, and **then** explain who they were and why they were in the plane to begin with." However in some cases you may not want to reveal too much at the beginning. Writing a good novel is about showing, not telling. Allow the reader to get to know your main character immediately, or at least in the first chapter. Remember to give your character realistic positive and negative qualities, strengths as well as weaknesses. Talk about what makes him or her tick. What makes them happy and what sends them off the deep end. You can also introduce your character's vocation, hobbies or education. Provide motivation. In other words, ask yourself what does your character want? Your reader should want that for them too. Place them in an unnatural environment, someplace where they're uncomfortable. Your novel can be an adventure, a mystery, a suspense thriller, a romance or horror story, etc.

Whatever you decide to write, it is important to keep your reader's interest. That's why you may want to start out with action. Action is a sure fire method to hook a reader. T.S. Eliot said, "If you start with a bang, you won't end with a whimper." Perhaps introducing your antagonist early on and the conflict or adversity he or she brings will do this for you. Use descriptive words. For example, instead of saying someone was hit by a punch, try saying they were *walloped*! See the difference? Studies show that if you can't keep your reader interested past the first 18 pages, you're not doing a good job. If the reader puts your book down, it's your fault not theirs. That's why you need to grab them right away and keep them interested by providing some type of action. Start taking your reader on an emotional roller coaster early and you'll keep them turning the pages until the very end. They'll always want to know what happens next. If you need help developing any of the things I've just discussed, please refer to the checklist I've included on the next page. Use it to develop one or each of your characters as well as the other elements you'll need.

<u>Writing Checklist</u>

Character Name _____

Major _____ Minor _____

Occupation _____

Physical Attributes: Race _____ Hair ____ Eyes _____

Height _____ Weight _____ Age _____ etc.

Protagonist _____ Antagonist _____

Plan/Goal/Motivation _____

Obstacle/Conflict 1: _____ 2: _____ 3: _____

Language/Dialect _____

Setting/Scenery: Sights ___ Sounds ___ Smells _____ etc.

Plot: Beginning _____ Middle _____ End _____

Writing Poetry

Perhaps no other genre of writing interests me more than poetry. I fell in love with it at an early age when my seventh grade literature teacher entered my name into a poetry reading contest. I read *Stopping by Woods on a Snowy Evening* by Robert Frost and won the contest. I earned the chance to represent my school in a citywide competition, and although I didn't win it, I was still proud of my accomplishment and was immediately smitten with poetry. I continued to read as well as write my own poetry through my high school years and throughout my four year stint in the U.S. Air Force. While in the Air Force, I wrote love poems for the other guys to mail home to their girlfriends. I can't tell you how many times my talents were requested by lonely young men who wanted something special and unique to send home. I probably solidified some engagements along the way, though I can't say for sure. I found out later in my career that Alex Haley, the award winning author of *Roots*, had done the same thing for his friends when he was in the military. I felt really special knowing that I have something in common with someone as famous as he.

It took me a while to realize that poetry was a gift that I'd been blessed with. I always looked at it as no big deal; I thought it was just something I had a knack for doing. It seemed to take no effort at all. It wasn't until after so many people were requesting copies of my work that I finally realized I must be on to something. I began printing my poetry on designer paper, matting and framing the poetry and selling them to individuals and stores. These were all poems I'd written for special occasions such as birthdays, holidays, weddings, anniversaries, graduations, even baby dedications. I was having great success. Then, someone suggested I compile some of my poetry and turn them into a book. I did, but unfortunately the results were nowhere near what I thought they would be.

It has been my experience that books of poetry don't sell too well. Now before you take this book and toss it to the other side of the room, let me explain why I made that statement. First, notice I said it has been *my* experience. It doesn't mean it will be yours too. I'm sure there are plenty of books of poetry written by poets that are doing quite well. But, unless your name is Maya Angelou or you have some other famous name, yours may be very difficult to promote. That's why I suggest that you sell your poetry individually rather than putting all of your poems in a book. You may even be able to create your own greeting cards. You can try to connect with an established greeting card company, but it may prove to be very difficult because most of them already have a team of writers. However, if you still feel confident about your work (as well you should) and think there's a market for it, then by all means go ahead and publish your book of poetry. This is one instance where I hope you prove me wrong. After all, the famous English poet Robert Graves once said, "There's no money in poetry, but then again there's no poetry in money either."

As I stated earlier, I suggest that you sell your poetry individually. You can do this by printing your work on designer paper as I used to do, and then have them individually matted and framed. This was working well for me, and then I discovered that I could write books. I even turned some of my poetry into children's books like Dr. Seuss did, and I have been very pleased with the results.

Selling your poetry individually works better from a monetary stand point, because if you do it right you can sell one poem for up to three times as much as you'd sell your book. Wouldn't you rather sell one poem and make more money than selling who knows how many in your book and making less? If someone sees your book of poetry on a coffee table, they may pick it up and read it, say a few complimentary words, then put it back down. But, if someone sees one of your poems beautifully displayed on a wall at someone's home or office, they'll want to know where they too can get one. Again, this may or may not be the case with you, but it has been my experience. You can also sell your poetry individually to magazines. This may help your cause if you still wish to pursue a publisher later. If you're writing poetry for children, check out magazines like *Highlights*, *Jack & Jill* and *Cricket*. Notice the style of poetry in them and check their websites for their submission guidelines.

Has anyone ever contacted you about placing one of your poems in an anthology? If they haven't and you don't know what an anthology is, let me explain. An anthology is a book that contains a collection of poetry from different people. Some companies contact poets and offer the opportunity – or "privilege," as they try to make it sound – to place a poem in an anthology. Of course, they'll invite you to do this at a price (normally $75 or more). Don't fall for it. Why should you pay to have your work placed in someone else's book? If they really think your work is good enough, believe me, they will offer to pay you, not the other way around. My motto is: If they want you to pay, run away. (More on this later.)

Memoirs and Autobiographies

Perhaps you'd like to write your own memoir or autobiography because you've lived quite an interesting life and you feel like the world needs to hear your story. Everyone has a story they'd like to tell, either about their childhood or something else they've gone through. While this may not be a bad idea, before you commit to it, I'd like you to consider the following information.

Remember the five W's I discussed earlier: who, what, when, where and why? Well there's another **W** I'd like to discuss and that is, "who cares?" As I just stated, everyone has a story. So what makes yours special? Why should anyone be interested in you? Unless you are a celebrity or someone else who's well known like an athlete, a politician or famous author (hopefully you're on your way to becoming one), most people won't care about your story. I'm not saying that you and your life story aren't just as important as any celebrity; I'm only saying that people like to read about people they're familiar with or those they want to know more about. Unless you really have something you think someone will be interested in, and something that will help them – such as overcoming an addiction, a dreadful disease, or perhaps surviving a near death experience – an autobiography or memoir may not be worth your time and effort.

If the advice I gave in the previous paragraph doesn't sit well with you and you're still dead set on writing your autobiography or memoir, all is not lost. There still may be a way to do it. Why not write it as a fictional story using the methods discussed earlier and changing the names? That way you can write it and no one will care whether you're a celebrity or not. Your story will be told, and you'll still get all the accolades and satisfaction from having written it.

Ghostwriting

Do you know the difference between being a writer and being an author? Did you know you don't have to be a writer to be an author? Most people think the two are one in the same, but they are not. A writer is someone who does just that, they write, either for themselves or for someone else. An author is the person whose name appears on the book or article.

According to a *New York Times* article, "On any given week, up to half the books on the nonfiction best selling list are written by someone other than the person whose name appears on the cover." Just because someone is an expert in a particular field doesn't necessarily mean they're a great writer. That's why the need for ghostwriters will always be in demand. If you're not too concerned about whether or not you get the credit for your writing, this may be a viable option for you.

To be a ghostwriter you simply have to find an expert or some celebrity who wants to write a book but just can't find the time, or doesn't have the necessary know-how to do it. Then, offer your services as a ghostwriter and write a contract charging them a flat fee, or an hourly, per page, or per chapter rate, as well as a percentage of their royalties. You can even choose to be paid in quarterly installments, such as a fourth in advance, another fourth when the book is halfway done, a fourth when you're three quarters done, and the final payment upon completion. Of course all of this is in return for your vow of silence and anonymity, thus the term "ghost." After you're done writing, the expert or celebrity's name will go on the cover, not yours. That's because even though you're the writer, they're the author. See my point?

Collaborations

In addition to becoming a ghostwriter, another option you may want to pursue is that of a collaborator. If you look at the word you can see it finds its roots in two words "co-" and "labor." That means you'll be working with someone else. In this case, your co-laborer or co-author should be someone who shares the same passion and desire as you when it comes to publishing your book. They do not, however, have to share the same expertise as you. It's perfectly fine if each of you bring different talents to the table, as long as you're both working towards the same goal.

When collaborating with another author it is important to designate each responsibility of the project. As with ghostwriting, you may want to sign a contract stating such duties and when they're to be completed. You may separately write a certain chapter or section, then bring it to the other to add or delete content. You will also need to decide whose name will go on the cover (yours or both), how the percentage of the royalty payments will be split (may not always be 50/50) and who owns the copyrights. Like a soft bed, collaborations are easy to get into but hard to get out of, so before you decide to do one, make sure you're going into it with both eyes open and with someone you know and trust.

Editing

Now that we've discussed the different facets of writing and how to write them, it's time to talk about what you'll have to do once they have been completed. Once you've completed your work (and in some cases during it), you'll need to do, or have someone else do, the most important task necessary before presenting your work to the public. That is the task of editing.

As you begin to write, keep in mind that you're going to make some mistakes. Some people like to refer to it as a rough draft or a first draft, but I like to call it a sloppy copy. Why do I call it a sloppy copy? Well, first of all because I'm a poet by nature and I like to make things rhyme, and secondly because I just think it sounds better than calling it a rough draft or even a first draft for that matter. You're free to call it whatever you like. I just like calling it a sloppy copy. You say to-*may*-to, I say to-*mah*-to. ☺

When you make mistakes, don't get discouraged. Notice I didn't say *if* you make mistakes, but *when* you make them. No one writes their book exactly the way they want the first time around whether they're an amateur or a professional. As a child I'm sure your parents discouraged you against being sloppy, and while in school your teachers probably did the same. However, this is one case where it's okay to be sloppy. Your sloppy copy will probably be riddled with mistakes, red check marks, lines drawn through text, etc. That's perfectly normal. After all, you're going through this for the first time, so don't feel bad about making mistakes. Everybody does it. I'm not saying that you should make mistakes on purpose. You should try to put forth your best effort. But, be assured that no matter how hard you try, you'll definitely have some mistakes when you're done. I can't tell you how many mistakes I made before I finished writing this book. But, after I finished, I went back and corrected them and I didn't do it alone. I had someone else look it over as well. This, as I'm sure you probably already know, is called editing. You should **never** be the only person to edit your work. Just as carpenters always need an inspector to look over their work before a house can be sold, you too need someone else to look over your writing when you're done. You can hire an editor, but make sure they charge you a flat rate, per word or per page, not per hour. Also be sure to ask what genre they specialize in. Editors who have a focus on self-help books are different from editors who edit children's books. Ask questions. Find out their fee and if they require payment in advance or in installments. Ask about their turnaround time, as well. In other words, how long will it take for them to get your work back to you? Asking these questions and getting a clear understanding will go a long way towards ensuring the quality of your book.

If you don't have the resources to hire an editor and you need to go the less expensive route, ask someone who's well-versed in the English language such as a high school English teacher or college professor to do it for you. Never try to edit your own work because your eyes will only see what you think is there rather than what really is. Sometimes the most obvious errors are the ones you'll miss most. That's why you must have someone else read over your work. However, if you're just dead set on doing it yourself, make sure you proofread your work on printed paper rather than on a computer screen. It's much easier to do it on paper than scrolling down a screen, and your eyes won't get as tired.

Conclusion

The steps I've listed in this chapter are merely suggestions. You may find that they may or may not work for you. After all, when it comes to writing a book, there's no clear cut way to tell you how to do it. At least I haven't found one. At the end of the day, the steps you decide to take in writing your book are totally up to you. What works for some people may not work for others. However you decide to do it, I hope the steps listed in this chapter have given you some sort of guideline on where and how to start, and how to complete your journey of becoming an author. Read on for more.

Chapter Summary

1) Test your children's book on children other than your own

2) The standard length for picture books is 24 to 32 pages

3) To get ideas, pay attention to your surroundings

4) Don't be afraid of doing research

5) Give your characters real attributes

6) Be sure to include the 5 W's

7) Never edit your own writing

Chapter Two

When to Write

Time is what we want most, but what we use worst.
— *William Penn*

So you've decided what you want to write and you have some idea of how to do it, now comes the challenge of deciding *when* to do it. I told you this journey wouldn't be easy. Between packing school lunches, going to work and sitting through board meetings, taking kids to soccer practice, helping with homework, preparing dinner and putting kids to bed, who has time to sit down and write? Well you do. That is if you really want to see your book on the shelf and in the hands of readers. You have to take time to do it. Your book is not going to write itself, you know. It will be written when you decide to do it and not a moment sooner.

When Should You Write?

Regardless of your daily schedule or regimen, finding the time to sit down and write is probably the hardest thing to do. With so much going on in life and having so many other things on your mind, it can be quite a task to transfer thoughts and ideas from your head to the paper or computer. Figuring out a time to do this is vitally important. As with deciding *what* to write, deciding *when* to write is equally as important and totally up to you. I know it's difficult to fit time into your busy schedule, but you *have* to do it. You have to be self-motivated and self-disciplined. Self-discipline is the bridge between the thought of writing your book and actually achieving it. So when should you do it? You have to find your "***write*** time." Here are a few suggestions.

     Some people like to wait until they're inspired to start writing. However, this can be difficult because inspiration can come to you anywhere and at anytime. If you like to write when you're inspired, knowing it can hit you at a moment's notice, you should always have a digital recorder handy or at least carry a pen and notepad wherever you go. You may even consider keeping that same pen and notepad or digital recorder on the nightstand next to your bed, because sometimes inspiration comes even when you're sleeping. If this happens, don't wait until morning when you get up to record or write your thoughts down. Chances are, your brain won't remember. Take advantage of the moment and write them down immediately. Even if it means you can't go back to sleep. Better to lose a little shut-eye than to lose an important thought.

     When deciding on the best time to write, do a bit of self-evaluation. Ask yourself: When do I feel the most productive? And, when does my mind feel at its creative peak? For some people, this may be early in the morning before the crack of dawn when everyone else is still asleep. For others, it may be at night after they've put the kids to bed and settled down. As I mentioned earlier, it takes self-motivation and self-discipline to do this. How bad do you want it? You have to be willing to make the sacrifice. I believe you should do something towards the completion of your manuscript every day. If you're not writing, perhaps you can spend time researching your particular subject. Whatever it is, make sure that you do at least one thing a day to propel you towards your goal of completing your manuscript.

How Much Time Should You Spend Writing?

After you decide what time of day is best for you to write, sometimes you may still feel like you have to force yourself to do it. Again this is where self-motivation and self-discipline come into play. Like almost any task, sometimes the hardest thing to do is get started. However, once you decide to get started and your creative juices start flowing, you may find it hard to put down the pen or walk away from the keyboard. Therefore, it may be a good idea to set goals and limits for your writing schedule. Your goal can be to write for at least an hour a day or until you've written a certain amount of words (maybe 1000 or so). It can be to finish at least one chapter a day or a week. Perhaps you can write for a certain period of time, walk away then come back and finish later. Try to set your own routine. Treat it as you would any job by taking breaks every now and then if you have to.

Whatever your goal is, don't set it too high or else you'll be disappointed in yourself if you don't meet it. This will only discourage you and may even cause you to quit, or at least lose valuable time before you decide to start writing again. Of course you shouldn't set your goal too low either as this may not keep you motivated. Be true to yourself because no one knows you and what you're capable of better than you.

While I can't tell you how long you should write, I do suggest that you write as often as you can, even if it's only a few minutes at a time between doing your chores or other activities. Take advantage of every free moment you get. You'll be amazed at how far in your writing process you'll get just by doing a little at a time. Make sure you do something (be it research or actual writing) towards the completion of your book as often as possible. Every little bit helps, and before you know it you'll start to feel a sense of accomplishment and your book will be finished. It's all about getting organized and making effective use of your time.

Where Should You Write?

Just as important as deciding when and how long to write, you should also decide where you'd like to write. I call this your "*write* place." Find a place to seclude yourself and get away from distractions. Distractions come along with the territory. They can come from anywhere; especially if you live in the city. It can come from the noise of traffic, your neighbors barking dog, the sound of a police or fire engine siren blaring, a plane flying overhead or even a train. It is often difficult to find a place of seclusion, but find one as soon as possible. Is there a place in your home that's quiet? Maybe you have a home office. What about using the break room at work after hours? Perhaps you might like to go to the park or to a library and work on your craft. I sometimes like to sit out on my deck in the early morning and write while listening to the birds sing. Wherever your place of solitude – be it at your home or somewhere else – make sure it offers enough peace to allow you to concentrate and stay focused. Concentration and staying focused are two of the most important things you'll need to master in order to complete your manuscript. If you master these two things, nothing will be able to distract you from your goal of being an author no matter where you decide to write. Finding a place of solitude will make your job a lot easier.

Writer's Block

So now you've decided when you'll write, where you'll write and for how long. But, what happens if after you've done all of this and you sit down to write and your mind is blank? Despite your best efforts, sometimes when you sit down to write you may have difficulty coming up with something. Your mind seems to draw a blank. What do you do when the words just won't seem to come out? This is what's commonly referred to as writer's block. When this occurs, don't panic and don't get discouraged. It happens to even the most experienced writers. Sometimes it may just be from a lack of focus, or maybe you're concerned that your work has to be perfect the first time around. Nothing can be further from the truth. Remember the sloppy copy we discussed earlier? My advice to you when you experience writer's block or a lack of focus is to write something anyway, even if it has nothing to do with what your book is about. You can always come back later and get rid of it. Writing something is better than sitting there staring at the paper or computer screen and writing nothing at all. Who knows, once the wheels get turning it may be hard to stop your fingers from dancing across the keyboard and before you know it, you're back on track. Don't let writer's block stop you from your goal of writing something every day.

Chapter Summary

1) Write when you feel most productive or creative

2) Always keep a pen and pad or digital recorder handy

3) Do something towards the completion of your book daily

4) Set a goal of how long you will write and when

5) Find a place to write that's free from distractions

6) Don't be discouraged by lack of focus (writer's block)

7) Don't think your writing has to be perfect the first time

Chapter Three

Designing a Cover

A good cover won't hide a bad book, but a bad cover will hide a good one.

- Dan Poynter

Now that you've completed your manuscript, and in some cases even before, you should start thinking about designing a cover for your book. Please don't take this decision too lightly because it could be the most important decision you'll make in determining the success or failure of your book.

People are visually stimulated, so they gravitate most towards what they see. Contrary to popular wisdom, most people can and do judge a book by its cover. It is for that reason that you must put a lot of thought into the design of yours. Most people spend about eight seconds browsing the front cover and approximately 15 seconds looking at and reading the back. People don't read books in the book store, but they do get a feel for whether or not they'd like to read them by perusing the cover. Your cover could decide whether a reader purchases your book, or simply looks at it and places it back on the shelf.

Although writing your book may be an individual effort, you'll still have to rely on others if you want to get the job done correctly. One of my favorite sayings is, "It takes teamwork to make the dream work," which is often attributed to Dr. Martin Luther King, Jr., and in order for you to have a great book you need to recruit some team members. One of the first team members you should recruit is a graphic artist or book designer to help design your book cover. If you want your cover to look professional and appealing, a good graphic artist or book designer should be able to do this for you. While you may have some idea of what you want your cover to look like, you may or may not be able to create it yourself. Graphic artists and book designers are trained in this area and can prove to be a great asset. You should be able to work closely with them to make sure that both of you are on the same page when it comes to the design of your cover. When deciding to hire a graphic artist or book designer, make sure to ask some of the same questions you asked your editor regarding payment terms, their credentials and turnaround time. Of course this only applies if your book is self-published. If your book is published by a mainstream publisher, they will make the decision of what your cover will look like and you won't have any input in it. (I'll talk more about this subject later.)

How Long Does it Take?

Whenever you decide to work with a graphic artist or book designer on the cover of your book, keep in mind that it may take a while. So start the process early. Start thinking about what you'd like your cover to look like and make sure you convey those thoughts clearly. Also, be sure to ask for an estimated completion date (they're busy people too you know). This will give you an idea of how soon you need to be finished with your manuscript if you haven't finished already. If you've already completed your manuscript and are ready to go to print with it, then make sure you give your graphic artist or book designer a timeline of when you'd like your cover to be ready. This will assure that both of you are on the same page. If necessary, get an agreement in writing stating when the work is to be done.

If you have photo shop software installed on your computer, you may be able to save yourself a lot of time and money by designing a cover yourself. You can use a personal photo of yours or one you've downloaded online. If you plan to do this, make sure it's at least 300dpi, otherwise it won't look as clear and vibrant when printed. Speaking of photos, several websites allow you to download images that you can use for the cover of your book. You may have to open an account or pay a small fee to use them, but I think they're well worth it. The two I like are www.google.com and www.dreamstime.com. Of course there are others you can use as well, such as Bing and Yahoo. If you're writing a children's picture book, it's a good idea to take two of your favorite illustrations from the inside of the book and use one of them for the front cover, and the other for the back cover. This will take the guess work out of your decision and make it less daunting.

Sizes and Materials

Books come in all different shapes, sizes and materials. Obviously a hardcover book is more durable than soft cover (paperback). But there are other factors to consider as well. Do you want the layout of your book to be printed in landscape (horizontal) or portrait (vertical) form? What size do you want it to be? Do you think you'd like it to be 5½ x 11, 8 x 10, 6 x 9, or some other size? The list goes on and on. That's another reason it's a good idea to visit your local library or book store and look at books similar to what you think you want yours to look like. Pay close attention to the different shapes, sizes and textures.

What about the pages? I use glossy pages for the children's picture books I write, because they're more durable and make the colors more vibrant. Kids love colors and the brighter they are, the better. However, using this type of paper means my production costs are a little higher than normal, but that's okay. You don't have to have your children's book or any other book for that matter printed on glossy paper like I do. The cost of paper may be your greatest expense when it comes to printing, so choose wisely. Most printers use 60lb paper and a stock between 40-70lbs. The heavier the weight, the thicker the book and the higher your cost will be.

Binding

There are several factors to consider when it comes to the binding of your book. Would you like it to be saddle-stitched, spiral bound or perfect bound? Of course, in some cases your binding options will depend on your page count. In most cases, soft cover books need to have a minimum of 64 pages in order to be perfect bound with a spine. You'll need to have it perfect bound if you want the title, your name and the name of the publishing company on the spine. This is the best route to go since books are displayed on the shelf with the spine facing the reader. This rule applies to both soft cover and hardcover books. If you're writing a chapter book and it doesn't quite meet the 64 page minimum, there are some things you can do to add pages to it. One is to add stories, pictures and quotations. Notice the word is "quotations", not "quotes". According to self-publishing expert Dan Poynter[2] (www.parapublishing.com) quotations make your text more interesting, seem more important and confirm your suggestions. He said they should be sprinkled throughout your text at the top or bottom of a page to reinforce your words. Another good technique is to add a questionnaire or summary at the end of each chapter like I've done with this book. Keep in mind, the more pages you use, the higher your costs will be.

If you can't find a way to apply any of the above techniques of adding pages to your book, you'll have to have it saddle-stitched (stapled) which is what you see with most pamphlets and it can only be soft cover. Of course that's fine too if that's all you want. Every book doesn't have to have a spine. Hardcover books don't have a minimum page count in order to have a spine as evidenced by most children's picture books only having 32 pages. Also with your hardcover book, you may choose to include a dust jacket, which is a picture of your cover on laminated paper that is placed over your book's hardcover.

Margins

When typing the text for the inside of your book, as well as for the front and back cover, remember to pay close attention to the margins. The size of the margins is an important factor in determining your book's readability both inside and out. Margins vary in size according to your book's design (hard or soft cover). If they're cut too close on the cover, it will cause some words not to show up when the book is printed and trimmed. The inside or gutter margin should be wider than the outside margin to put less stress on the binding and spine when the book is opened. They normally work best when the top, bottom and outside measure .05 inch and .75 for the inside margin. The printing company, and your graphic artist or book designer should be better able to help you determine what's best according to the size and dimensions of your book.

Page Layout

As with determining your margins, another important factor to consider is that of the page layout for your book. Obviously you'll want to make sure the pages coincide with the dimensions of the size and cover, but there are other factors to consider, as well. First, as a general rule (but not always), if you're writing a chapter book, all chapters should begin on the right (as facing the reader), not the left. This should be done consistently throughout your book, even if a chapter finishes on the right and you have to leave the next page blank. This can be used as a space-filler and to add more pages to your book. Start your page numbers on the right, as well. This means your odd number pages should always be on the right and the even numbers on the left. Although we read and count from left to right, when it comes to writing a book, you'll find that things are usually done a little differently.

Choosing a Title

As I stated earlier, choosing a cover is one of the most important decisions you'll have to make regarding the success or failure of your book. In addition to the graphic design of your cover, you'll want your book to have a good title. After all, in many cases the title is what prompts a reader to pick up a book in the first place. It is for that reason that you need to choose your words carefully. A catchy phrase or a play on words is a good way to pique a reader's interest. Does the tone of the title match the tone of your book? Does it give the reader some idea of what your book is about? These are questions you should ask yourself when trying to decide on a good title.

A title cannot be copyrighted; still you may not want to use one that's already been taken. So how do you find out if the title you're thinking of has already been used? One way is to do a search for it on Amazon.com. There you'll find a list of all books that are currently in print as well as out-of-print. If your book is the same as or even similar to another book, this could cause some confusion for readers whenever they're searching for yours. This is where a good sub-title can make the difference and distinguish your book from others.

While your title should be short (no more than five to seven words), your sub-title can be longer and more descriptive. The title and sub-title work hand in hand. Together they should leave no question as to what your book is about. Of course, sometimes it is okay to leave the reader guessing what your book is about. This may intrigue them and make them want to open the book to see what's in store. You'll want to spark an, *I wonder what this is about* reaction in a potential reader, as opposed to a *So what?* reaction.

When placing your title on the cover, what typeface or font size should you use? Well again, the choice is up to you. What color should the letters be? Do you want them to be bold and decorative, or simple and plain? Do you want to place your title and subtitle at the top or bottom of the cover? How about the placement of your name? All of these are questions you should ask yourself. If you're not sure what you should do, again I suggest perusing your local bookstore or library to see what other books that are similar to yours look like.

Sometimes the subject of your book will determine what the typeface on the cover should look like. For example, if you're writing a horror story, the typeface should be formed differently than it would if you're writing a romance novel. Whatever typeface you decide on, make sure it's visually appealing and adds to, not detracts from, the overall look of the cover. People are attracted to what they see. If your cover isn't visually appealing, it may not get picked up at all. You must have something that will make people stop and take notice. The words, the typeface, and the image on your cover should all complement each other. Dan Poynter says, "A good cover won't hide a bad book, but a bad cover will hide a good one." This is great advice for beginners as well as professionals.

Capitalization

When creating your title, keep in mind that every word does not have to be capitalized. Although some authors have done this (myself included), it is not necessary. Some authors will even capitalize every letter in their title. This too is unnecessary, but it's a matter of choice. According to Arlene Miller[3], "The Grammar Diva," the standard rules when it comes to capitalization are to always capitalize the first and last words of a title, and never capitalize words like *a, and,* and *the* unless they are the first or last words of a title. Also, words like *for, and, nor, but, or, yet,* or *so* do not have to be capitalized unless they are the first or last words of a title.

Should Your Picture Be on the Cover?

Are you famous? Are you a celebrity? Do you have name recognition? Whether you answered no to one, or all, of these questions, your picture does not need to be on the front cover of your book. Even if your book is about you, it's probably not a good idea to put your picture on the cover unless you're a well known celebrity, politician, or some other type of recognizable personality. In that case, your face is your calling card. It's your brand. But if you don't fit into any of these categories, it's best to leave your picture off the front cover. If you're not a celebrity and still want to put your picture on the front cover (as I did on one of my books), the choice is totally up to you.

The back cover is different. While placing your picture on the front cover may not be a good idea, it is acceptable to put it on the back cover. When doing so, you should make it a small headshot and place it either in the bottom left or right corner, opposite your barcode and ISBN (which I will discuss in the next chapter). It may be placed in the top left or right corner as well.

In addition to your picture being on the back cover, you should also include testimonials or a brief synopsis of what your book is about. Testimonials are a great selling tool because they tell what others think about you and your book. It's one thing to brag on yourself, but it's quite another when someone else does it. Testimonials build people's trust in you. They should tell the results someone got from reading your book, not just what a good read it was. Some authors even write the testimonials themselves and ask people to sign off on them.

If you want to write a synopsis on the back cover of your book, be sure to make it saleable. In other words, make sure it has a hook to grab the reader right away and keep them reading. Remember, people normally spend about eight seconds looking at and reading the front cover, and about 15 seconds reading the back. Use the front cover to get them in the door and the back cover to close the sale. It should make the reader want to know more. For example, if you're writing a self-help book, then give readers a reason to buy your book by listing its benefits using bullet points. People want to know what's in it for them. Each bullet point should start with an action verb such as, "Learn how to..." or other words like, *Improve*, *Discover*, *Start*, etc. As I mentioned earlier, looking at other books and noticing the way other authors use these words will give you some idea of how you can use them, as well.

What Needs To Be In Your Book

In between the front and back covers of your book you obviously should have the pages with your story written on them. But, that's not all. You'll also need other pertinent information called front and back matter.

Front matter consists of things like your title page with copyright date and other information on the back, such as publisher and printing company information. Your contact information and the ISBN of your book should also be on the back of the title page. In addition to this, your front matter can also include a dedication page, an introduction page, an acknowledgment page to thank all the people who helped you along the way, and a foreword. Of course, if you're writing a chapter book you'll also need a table of contents.

At the end of the book, after the story and before the back cover, you should have your back matter. This includes an index, an appendix, an epilogue, an about the author page, an order form for your other books, if applicable, and an afterword page. Of course you may or may not need all the pages I suggested for your front and back matter. But again, as I've stated repeatedly, it's a good idea to take a look at other books and follow their patterns.

Chapter Summary

1) Most people will spend eight seconds perusing the front cover and 15 seconds looking at the back cover

2) Choose your title carefully

3) As Dan Poynter stated, "A good cover won't hide a bad book, but a bad cover will hide a good one."

4) Photos need to be at least 300 dpi

5) Place your picture on the back cover, not the front

6) Be sure to include front and back matter

7) Make sure the typeface of your title matches the subject of your book

Section 2

How to Publish Your Book

Chapter Four
Traditional Publishing

There are three difficulties in authorship: to write anything worth publishing – to find honest men to publish it – and to get sensible men to read it.
— Charles Caleb Cotton

Now that you've learned how to write your book, when to write it and what the cover and contents should contain, it is now time to publish it. With so many publishing options available today it can be difficult deciding which route to choose. However, after reading this chapter, hopefully you'll have an idea of how to proceed with confidence.

Pursuing a Publisher

As with every industry, publishing has seen its share of changes over the years. After all, no industry can hope to survive without change. One of, if not the biggest change in the publishing industry is the act of self, or indie (independent), publishing, which is what this book is mainly about. However, I wouldn't do you justice if I didn't give you information on how to pursue a traditional publisher if that's something you're interested in doing.

The main thing to decide when pursuing a traditional publisher, like anything else, is where to start. With so many publishing houses to choose from, deciding on the right one can be daunting to say the least. However, there is a place you can start that's not so intimidating: purchase a copy of the latest edition of the *Writer's Market*. This book is a new author's best friend. Why? Because it contains everything a new author, and even a well established one, needs to know when it comes to pursuing a publisher. Each edition is updated annually with the latest information on publishing companies, editors and even agents.

What makes the *Writer's Market* such a great resource is its lists of all publishers according to subjects and other categories. For example, if your book is a mystery novel, the *Writer's Market* will have a list of publishers that accept books dealing with that genre. But it doesn't stop there. It provides pertinent information such as whether or not the particular publisher you're thinking of sending your manuscript to accepts work from first time authors and whether or not you need an agent. It will also tell you whether or not the publisher accepts books of poetry, or in the case of a children's book (use *The Children's Writer's and Illustrator's Market*), whether or not they accept picture books or chapter books. In addition to all of this, the *Writer's Market* will give you the publisher's contact information, tell you whether or not the publisher accepts multiple submissions (that is sending your manuscript to more than one publisher at a time), as well as give you their submission guidelines. What more can you ask for? This is a must have for **any author** who wishes to develop a relationship with a publisher.

The Query Letter

If you find that you meet a certain publisher's criteria, submit your manuscript to them. Again, the publisher will give you specific instructions on how to do this via their submission guidelines. The first thing you will need to do is send them a query letter. The word query means to ask, so what you're doing in your query letter is basically asking a publisher if they'd like to see your manuscript. In it you'll give details about your manuscript as well as talk about your credentials. In other words, you'll have to toot your own horn and you shouldn't be afraid to do so. Tell them about your experiences and what qualifies you to write your book. Talk about any awards or other accolades you've received as a result of your writing abilities. Think of it as sort of a resume. The publisher wants to know why they should publish your book, what makes it special and why anyone should care.

Like your book, the first paragraph of your query letter needs to have a hook to grab the publisher's interest and make them want to read your manuscript. It only needs to be one page long. You don't have to elaborate or give too many details. Give just enough to make the publisher want to know more. Make sure it is free of any typos or spelling errors. You may use bullet points if you like, but be sure you stick to one main idea.

When writing your query letter it is important that you address it to the right person. This could be the person listed in the *Writer's Market* (that's why it's a good idea to research it annually), or it may be someone you met at a particular conference you attended. Speaking of conferences, it's a good idea to attend as many writing conferences as you can, because chances are you'll have an opportunity to meet a lot of publishers, editors, and even agents there. Be sure to get their contact information and send your query letter to them as soon as possible.

The second paragraph of your query letter is where you give more details about your manuscript. Here, you will tell the publisher how far along you are if you're not finished with it yet, and give them a possible completion date and word count. If you are finished with your manuscript, be sure to let the publisher know that you're ready to send it to them immediately if necessary.

At the end of your query letter be sure to thank the publisher and let them know that you're looking forward to hearing from them soon. Be sure to include all your contact information, full name, home and email address, as well as your home and cell phone number.

Writing a Proposal

While a query letter is normally submitted for a book that has already been written, a proposal letter is submitted for one that has not. It is for that reason that they are usually submitted by more established writers since, unless you're writing non-fiction, it is a difficult sell for a new writer to pique an editor's interest in something that hasn't been completed.

I have a friend who is an established children's author. His name is Charles Ghigna[4], AKA "Father Goose." He has had dozens of books published by a major publisher. He says when you're writing a book proposal, you should make them short, including only a few sentences about your book. According to Mr. Ghigna, you should also include the title and subtitle of your proposed book, along with a brief description of it, and it should be done via email. He also says that sometimes your subtitle itself will explain a summary of your book. Finally, he adds that you should include your name, a brief list of your publication credits, and the age of the audience for whom your book is intended. Here is a sample of one of his proposal letters along with a link to find book editors.

GOODNIGHT NIGHTTIME, HELLO DAY!

By Charles Ghigna

Summary: (32-page Picture Book)

Baby Bear wakes up and strolls outside to play. In his quest to find a friend, he engages other woodland playmates he meets in a game of hide and seek. They follow him along his journey. He finally comes to a brook, looks in and sees his reflection, and thinks he sees another bear! He falls in and realizes his new best friend is himself. By the end of the day Baby Bear has made many new friends, including himself. He falls asleep dreaming about meeting another new friend tomorrow.

Visit www.underdown.org to find children's book editors.

Submitting Your Manuscript

When submitting your manuscript to a publisher, make sure you type it on plain white 8½ x 11 paper using a standard font. On the first page, in the top left corner, type your name, address, email and phone number. Make sure this is single spaced. In the top right corner, type the approximate word count of your manuscript. This does not have to be accurate. Space down to about the middle of the page and type your title centered, followed by your name. After that, you can begin typing your manuscript double spaced on the same page. You do not have to type the page number on the first page; however, you do need to type it at the top of each subsequent page along with the title next to it. Be sure to leave a one inch margin. Do not bind or staple your manuscript. Instead, use a rubber band or a large paperclip to keep the pages together. Of course you don't have to bind the pages at all if you don't want to since they all should be numbered anyway. Upon completion of all this, your manuscript is ready to be mailed to a publisher, unless the publisher indicates that they'd rather have your manuscript submitted via email. If you are sending it via the U.S. Post Office or any route other than email, always be sure to include a self addressed stamped envelope (SASE).

Once you've submitted your manuscript, it becomes a matter of playing the waiting game. How long will you have to wait? Well, that depends on the publishing company. It could take up to three or four months if not longer for them to get back in touch with you. Most publishers will have this information listed in the *Writer's Market* as well, so reference that guide to get a general idea of when you can expect to hear back. If you haven't heard from them within the timeframe they have listed, it's perfectly okay to contact them to find out the status of your manuscript.

If you find that the publisher is holding your manuscript longer than the time they have listed in their guidelines, this may not be a bad thing. They may be holding it longer to make a final decision or to write back to you with a revision or some other suggestion.

Manuscripts that are returned too quickly or before the guideline suggests are usually rejection letters.

Dealing with Rejection

Rejection is something we've all had to deal with at some time or another in our lives. It's quite common in the publishing arena and as with all the other rejections we've encountered, it doesn't feel good. Well, don't take it personal. It happens even to the best writers. Accept it and move on. Don't let it keep you from moving forward and don't allow it to put a damper on your creativity.

Most publishers have a standardized rejection statement saying that they can't use your work at this time. This is no reflection on you or your work, so don't take it personal. They didn't say your work was bad, they just said they couldn't use it at this time. Just because they couldn't use it, doesn't mean another publisher can't. Some publishers may even make a few suggestions on how you can make your manuscript better. If you receive a rejection letter, don't be disappointed, be encouraged that at least the publisher took the time to read your work. I like to think the glass is always half full in this business. So again, don't let rejection letters discourage you, even if you receive 20 or more. If you really want to have your book published, keep submitting your work and make whatever changes they have suggested. Eventually your persistence will pay off.

Getting Accepted

At the opposite end of being rejected is being accepted. The publisher will probably give you a personal call congratulating you. If this happens, what do you do? Well, after you pick yourself up from the floor, calm down and think about how you should proceed in signing a contract. The publisher will make you an offer and it's up to you to decide whether you want to accept it or not. Again, don't get too excited. You don't have to accept the first contract offer they present to you.

The contract will usually state the terms of the agreement such as the amount you will be paid in advance and your percentage of royalty payments from sales of your book. Most royalty payments range from 6-10% of net profits. It will also state who will retain the copyrights as well as any other rights you're entitled to should your manuscript be used for a movie or electronic media. Dealing with all this information can be confusing. Therefore, you may want to enlist the help of an attorney. Just any attorney will not be suitable. Make sure you find one who you can trust that deals with literary contracts.

Should You Hire an Agent?

As I mentioned in the previous paragraph, trying to deal with the terms of a literary contract can be confusing. That's why you may want to hire an agent to do it for you. Literary agents know all the ins and outs of contracts and can negotiate a better deal for you. Of course, it comes at a price, so it's up to you to decide whether you can afford one or not. Agents may be able to get your work into publishing houses that you normally wouldn't be able to on your own. I say they *may* be able to do this because just like authors, sometimes agents get rejected too.

When working with an agent, make sure it's someone you can meet with in person. Never do any negotiating with them over the phone and be sure to get everything in writing. Remember they work for you and it's in their best interest to do a good job because they don't get paid unless you do. Also, as with a publishing house, you don't have to sign a contract with the first agent that comes along. Feel free to shop around.

Agents can be found at writer's conferences, the *Writer's Market,* or by going online to The Association of

Authors Representatives, Inc. at www.aaronline.org. Loriann Hoff Oberlin[5] suggests in her book, *Writing for Quick Cash,* that another way to find an agent is to talk to an author who has one. She says you can talk to the agent but don't use the author's name unless they've given you permission to do so. She also suggests calling the publishing company that published a particular book you like and ask who represented the author.

Other Factors to Consider

After your manuscript is accepted and you've signed a contract, whether you decide to use an agent or not, it may take up to a year and a half or more before your book is printed. That's because most publishers work on an 18-month production cycle. And again, this doesn't start until after all negotiations have been agreed upon and your contract has been signed. Also, most of the time the publisher, not you, will make the final decision on what the cover of the book and any illustrations will look like. They may even change the title without your input.

Another thing you need to know is that publishers have three selling seasons each year. That means they normally only keep a book on the shelf for four months before replacing it. They initially print about 5000 copies and if the sales are good, the book is reprinted and the publisher will spend more money to promote it further. However, if the sales aren't good, the book is pulled off the shelf and remaindered (sold off cheaply) to make room for other new books. I don't mean to end this chapter on such a solemn note. I only want to make sure I give you all the details about publishing I can think of so you will be well informed regardless of the decision you choose to make.

Chapter Summary

1) Check the *Writer's Market* to find publishers

2) Write an effective query letter

3) You can submit your manuscript to more than one publisher at a time

4) Getting rejected doesn't mean your work isn't good

5) Publishers work on an 18 month production cycle

6) You may or may not need an agent

7) You don't have to accept the first offer presented to you

Chapter Five
Other Choices in Publishing

Thank your readers and the critics who praise you, and then ignore them. Write for the most intelligent, wittiest, wisest audience in the universe: Write to please yourself.
-Harlan Ellison

Did you know that there are several ways to publish your book? Most people only think of the traditional way we discussed in the last chapter, but there are various other options you can explore. In this chapter I will explain what they are. Hopefully, after reading this chapter you'll have a better understanding and knowledge of the alternative methods that are available.

We've already discussed the first option of publishing for most people, that of pursuing the traditional route. If you don't want to pursue one of the big traditional publishers in New York, you can look for a mid-sized or niche publisher for a certain genre. You can also hire a literary agent to solicit your work to a publisher like I mentioned earlier. In addition to these options, there's another type of publishing I'd like to introduce you to. That is the art of Print-on-Demand, or POD as it is sometimes called.

Print-on-Demand

As I stated in the previous chapter, when you go the traditional publishing route, initially only about 5000 copies of your book will be printed, and of those, chances are that less than half may sell. For a first time author this can be disappointing. With print-on-demand publishing you can sign a contract with a fee-based company that will digitally print a certain amount of books for you. This can reduce your printing costs substantially and eliminate having to store large quantities of books in your garage, basement or attic. Remember, with traditional publishing it may take up to 18 months or more to see your book in print, whereas with print-on-demand you can have it done much sooner. Print-on-demand companies offer authors several packages to choose from. You get to choose which package you like and as your book sells, you'll collect a royalty percentage (which will be explained in your contract). However, be aware that the POD company owns the rights to your book for a period of time. This will also be specified in the contract. In addition to the initial fee charged for printing, there will be charges for obtaining an ISBN and copyright registration as well as charges for designing the book's cover.

Before you consider going the POD route, there are some other factors you may want to consider, as well. When most people think about purchasing a book, a POD website is probably the last place they consider looking.

That's because most of the people who visit these websites are authors like you who are looking to sell books, not buy them. Also, when a reviewer finds out your book has been published by a POD company, they often tend to not look at it. Another thing to consider is most bookstores don't like dealing with POD books because authors have to price them higher than normal to compensate for the high commission the POD company charges them. Also, most POD companies don't offer editing services unless you pay extra for specific packages. That means they will print exactly what you send them and what you're willing to pay for. This may or may not be acceptable to you. I suggest you weigh all your options after doing your research.

Vanity or Subsidy Publishing

Another form of publishing that's become popular with first time authors and some who've been frequently rejected by traditional publishers is vanity or subsidy publishing. Some of the companies who offer this are Xlibris, Author House, iUniverse and Lulu. I consider these companies to be publishing predators and I'll tell you why. First of all, they want you to pay them to publish your book. Remember my motto: If they want you to pay, run away. Have you ever heard the expression, "If something sounds too good to be true, it usually is"? This is what I think of when it comes to vanity or subsidy publishers. You may often see their ads in magazines or online offering promises they rarely keep. Vanity publishers pretend to be publishers but really they're not.

Aren't publishers supposed to make their profits from selling books? Not so with vanity or subsidy publishers. They make profits by swindling money from unsuspecting and naïve authors who desperately want to see their books in print. Think about it. Whoever publishes your book should care whether or not your book is successful because they have a vested interest in it, wouldn't you think? It should be a win-win relationship for all parties involved. This is not so with vanity publishers. After they receive their money from you, they couldn't care less whether your book succeeds or not. They've already gotten what they came for. Their only motive is to take advantage of people and make money. I'm all for companies making money, but the methods they use are ridiculous. I think they should be illegal, but they're not.

Here's another way to look at it. If a vanity publisher thinks your book is so great (and that's what they'll tell you), they should pay *you* to publish it, not the other way around. After all, that's why celebrities and other people with name recognition who I mentioned earlier never pay anyone to publish their books. The publisher pays them in advance, in addition to offering them royalties because they know they can make money off of their stories. The publisher is basically buying a brand (the celebrity's name) because they know they can profit from it alone if nothing else.

Another reason to stay away from vanity or subsidy publishers is because even after they print your book, the promotion of it is still up to you. You don't see celebrities or well known authors promoting their own books unless they're on TV or some other media outlet, do you? And who do you think arranged for them to be there? You guessed it, their publisher, agent or someone else who has a vested interest in the success of their book. Furthermore, even after you've finished paying the vanity press for printing your books, you'll still have to share a large percentage of the profits from each book sale with them. You won't really start getting your money back until after you've sold a certain amount of copies, usually around 5000 or so. Also, whenever you want more books, you'll have to buy them from the vanity publisher albeit at a discount. This in my opinion is highway robbery.

You may ask, isn't this the same as the POD companies we just discussed? Well it is, only worse. Like POD, a lot of bookstores don't like dealing with vanity press authors because of the cost involved. And, like POD, vanity publishers will only do editing if you're willing to pay more for their package. Also like POD, reviewers don't really like reviewing their books either.

If your goal is simply to see your book in print and not profit from it, then these companies are right for you. But, if you're serious about becoming a respectable and established author, you need to stay as far away from them as you can. With so many advances in technology lately, it's become easier for anyone to become a published author. However, it's become easier for new authors to be taken advantage of, as well. Inexperienced authors are at a tremendous disadvantage when it comes to publishing and these companies know it. So, before you sign a contract, do your homework and research to make sure you don't sign something you don't understand or, even worse, something you don't want. Now before you get upset, let me say that I'm sure there are some people who have benefitted from vanity and subsidy publishers. After all, there are exceptions to every rule. I just don't see the point in paying someone else to do what you can do yourself. Furthermore you're paying them twice, once to print your book then again to purchase more of them to sell.

To further support my view, on the next page I've included an article recently posted by Publisher Services, an authorized agent of US ISBN. You may contact them at:

875 N. Michigan Ave #2950
Chicago, IL 60611 Phone: 1-800-662-0701 x250

Independent Self-Publishers Beware

Posted on: February 11th, 2014

According to a recent report by Bowker, the number of self-published titles was up 60% in 2012. In 2011 246,921 titles were self-published compared to 391,768 in 2012. Since 2007, there has been a 422% increase in the number of independently self-published books.

Now that self-publishing has officially arrived, the number of new companies offering services to independent authors has exploded. As with any "unregulated industry", it is extremely important you thoroughly research companies before signing a contract or spending a dime. Although the internet is the primary research tool, there is a tremendous amount of misinformation and fraudulent companies preying on the new authors.

Before the digital book revolution, most of the industry's complaints were directed towards "vanity presses". There were countless horror stories of how authors paid money to a vanity press for book printing, warehousing, and distribution services and never received a dime in royalties. In many cases, these companies went out of business or did absolutely nothing to promote their clients' books. Today, there are even more companies offering book publishing services and many who prey on self-publishers. Before you engage with a publishing service company, we recommend you do the following:

- Directly contact the company by phone. Ask questions about how long they have been in business and if they can provide actual referral contacts (don't depend solely on web posted testimonials).
- Check with the local Better Business Bureau (BBB)
- If you are researching a publishing company, ask to see multiple recent successful titles. A few companies might have hit it big with a single title and the remaining 99% of their clients only sold a handful of books.
- Inquire about how royalties are paid and tax information is provided. We just heard a story how BookBaby does not provide 1099misc tax forms for royalties paid.
- Perform a Google search with the companies name and add the term complaint. This might bring up stories or posts by disgruntled customers.
- Check the company's Twitter and Facebook posts. Many unhappy clients use Twitter or Facebook feeds as a mechanism to air their problems.

Lastly, if you are considering using a book publisher please visit Preditors & Editors. This is a research site which denotes companies which they have received complaints. Obviously, if you are asked to sign a contract, please read it very carefully and try to get legal assistance before you sign. Be very wary of any contract which cannot be easily terminated or involves exclusivity. Please follow our blog posts at www.isbn-us.com/publisher-talk/ .

Self-Publishing

Of all the publishing methods I've mentioned so far, I think self, or indie (independent) publishing, is the best. Why do I say this? Well one reason is that it's what I prefer. I have used it with all of my books so far. Secondly, I just feel it's the best option for someone just starting out. When I first started writing books, I sent my manuscripts to several publishers I'd found in the *Writer's Market*, and some I'd met while attending writing conferences. I did this for more than a year and received countless rejection letters. Like most people, I didn't like the feeling of being rejected so many times. Being **rejected** left me feeling **dejected**, which, believe it or not, **injected** me with a lot of confidence. I knew that having my books published was something I really wanted to do, and I wasn't going to let a little thing like being rejected stop me.

There have been many authors who started out as self-publishers before getting their big break with a major publisher. John Grisham, Mark Twain and Stephen King are just a few names that come to mind right off hand. I also have a friend who really helped me a lot when I first decided that I wanted to write books. Her name is Vanessa Davis Griggs (www.vanessadavisgriggs.com). A Christian novelist, she self-published her books before they were picked up by a publisher.

Self-publishing gives you total control of your work. You don't have to worry about giving someone else a percentage of your profits because you get to keep 100% of them yourself. Of course you have to take on all the responsibilities of being a publisher like printing, marketing and distribution which can be a lot of work and in many cases quite costly. But it doesn't have to be. With the advent of the Internet and by using some of the methods I mentioned earlier, self-publishing has become more and more popular and less expensive. All it takes is a little effort and research on your part, and if done properly, in the end it will be well worth it. Who knows, your book may even be picked up by a major publisher after they see it on the shelf and take note of its success.

As I've said before, I subscribe to the belief that teamwork makes the dream work. You need to enlist the help of a team of individuals to handle the other duties needed to produce your book while you concentrate on the most important thing, writing it. These duties include (but are not limited to): typesetting, printing and binding, cover design, illustrations (if needed), marketing and distribution. Of course if you're well versed in any of these areas, you can do it on your own to cut down on your costs. Oh, and don't forget the art of editing and proofreading. As I mentioned earlier, that's something you should never do on your own.

Self-publishing means you are the franchise. That means you wear all the hats of author, publisher, promoter, agent, marketing director and all other duties assigned. It is up to you to make things happen. The success or failure of your book rides on your shoulders and no one else's. You'll have to do the same thing a publisher would do if they decided to publish your book, and you'll have to use your own money to do it. It may sound like this is the same as vanity, subsidy or POD publishing, and in a way it is because you still have to pay to have it done. But, there are several major differences as well. Remember, in POD and vanity publishing you have to pay the company plus give them a percentage of your sales. In self-publishing you don't have to do that. You keep all the profits for yourself. Also, with POD and vanity publishing, you're paying for the printing and publishing of your book. While it's okay to pay for printing, you should never pay anyone to publish your book, except yourself of course. Remember I said earlier that if a publishing company thinks your book is great, they'll offer to pay you, not the other way around.

As for the promises the vanity publisher makes, do you really have any way of knowing whether or not they're going to keep them? Do you have the time and are you willing to make sure they're doing what they said they would do? Again, with self-publishing you won't have this problem because you're the one who will have to keep up with what's being sold to who, when and where. You can do this by connecting with local or national distributors or by using mail order options such as Amazon.com. To view some of the differences between publishing and self-publishing, see the chart by Dan Poynter I've included on the next page.

Traditional Publishing	Self-Publishing
Must draft a proposal	No wasted time
18 months to get off press	5 weeks to print the book
Advance against royalties	No advance or royalties
No royalties for 2-3 years	Money flows in 30 days
Little promotion by publisher	Assured promotion
Lose control of book	Keep control of book
Book in stores only 4 months	Book sells forever
No revision allowed	Always up to date
Fewer tax deductions	More business expenses
Good possibility of rejection	No rejection
You only have to write and promote	Must run business too

Printing Your Book

So how much will it cost to have your book printed? Well the answer to that question depends on a number of factors such as the company you decide to use, its location, the size and material of your book (hardcover or soft cover), binding, paper poundage (40-70), the number of pages, cover poundage (laminated or uv coating), inside text and or pictures (color or black and white), and the number of copies you want to have printed. The more you have printed, the cheaper the cost per copy. The costs involved with these all important factors will go a long way towards determining the profitability of your book. The more it costs to have your book printed the more you'll have to charge someone to purchase it.

Since you'll be the one footing the bill, choosing the best printing company to use for your book is something you should give very careful consideration. As with making any major purchase, you should probably check with at least three companies before making your final decision. If you are comparing domestic and international companies, you'll find that their costs may differ drastically; especially when it comes to shipping. Of course you'll probably be able to reduce these costs by using a local printing company or one that's within a closer proximity to your residence. Regardless of which company you decide to use, make sure they produce quality work. Ask to see samples before you make your decision. After all, it's your product and your reputation that's going to be presented to the public, so you need to make sure they meet your standards.

Other Options

With the help of the Internet, printing and publishing your own book has never been easier. Amazon.com is a great tool to use when it comes to getting your book out to the public. After your book is printed, go to www.amazon.com/advantage and register your book in the online catalog. This will allow customers to log on to Amazon and order your book just as they would any other book from an established author or publisher. Amazon will keep 45% of each book sold while you will receive the other 55%. Again this is why you need to price your book accordingly so you will still be able to make a profit, even if it isn't 100%. A little bit of something is always better than a whole lot of nothing.

Another option you may want to consider when dealing with Amazon is their POD service called Create Space where you can upload a pdf file of your book. You can even include pictures, but keep in mind they must be at least 300dpi for clarity. Once your file is created, you will be able to order as many copies of your book as you like at a very affordable price. Should you need it, Create Space will even help with the design of your cover and the issuing of an ISBN. They also offer standard and expanded distribution options you should consider to help make your book available to more readers. This POD service offers the same options I mentioned earlier so like I said, make sure you do your research before deciding whether or not it's right for you. Visit www.createspace.com for more details.

EBooks

Ebooks are the wave of the future, or as of now, the present. With its advent, no longer do readers have to lug around heavy loads of books in their book bags or take up valuable space on shelves. Of course you will always have people who still prefer the look, feel and smell of a physical book. But for others, ebooks are the way to go. One reason is because of their convenience and immediacy. It only takes a few clicks of a mouse and your book is on someone's screen immediately. Another reason why a lot of people enjoy ebooks is, as I just mentioned, they're a lot easier to store. You can have thousands of books right at your fingertips by downloading them to your Kindle or other e-reader device.

Speaking of the Kindle, it is another tool that you can use to sell your books. To use Amazon Kindle Direct Publishing, go to www.kdp.amazon.com, and follow the simple steps to upload your file in MS Word or pdf format. Amazon will send you an email letting you know when your book is available, normally within 24 hours. Amazon will even post the English version of your ebook on its international websites in Europe (UK, Germany, France, Spain and Italy).

KDP Select is a program that allows you to upload your books and sell them for $2.99 or more. If you do this, you will receive a 70% profit each time someone downloads your book to their kindle device. Amazon Prime members can borrow your book for free, and when they do, you'll also receive a small royalty. You can also offer a free giveaway of your book. This is a great tool to use, however one thing that deters some authors from using KDP Select is the fact that it gives Amazon exclusive electronic rights to your book for 90 days. That means you won't be able to make it available on other devices like the Apple ipad or Barnes and Noble's Nook until after your 90 days have expired. After that, you're free to upload it to as many other devices as you would like. Despite this exclusivity, this has still proven to be the method of choice for many authors. You can also use www.smashwords.com and www.lightningsource.com for your ebook conversions. Again, these are the sites you'll use to make your book available on other devices in addition to Amazon's Kindle. When you visit these websites, you will see the individual guidelines and royalty payment structures.

Formatting your text in an ebook for correct readability can be frustrating because there are so many different types of devices. Split paragraphs and text behind images are common problems. You may want to hire someone else to do this for you if you don't have much experience doing it yourself. Dan Poynter is an author and self-publishing expert whose opinion is highly respected in the industry. As a matter of fact, most of the information I've learned over the years and even shared in this book comes from reading his monthly e-newsletter (Sign up at www.parapublishing.com). A free subscription is a must for anyone desiring to publish their own book. In his book entitled, *Writing Your Book: Cashing in on publishing faster, easier and cheaper,* he offers this advice when converting your book to an ebook: "In MS Word for the text, select a sans serif typeface such as *Arial, Tahoma* or *Verdana* because the sans serif will look better on a computer screen than serif type. Don't worry about headers or page numbers and don't add page numbers to your table of contents. Also, you don't have to add an index because readers can use the search option to find anything they're looking for." Some authors decide to publish their books in ebook form first before publishing them in print. That's because it's a lot less costly to do so.

Recently I've learned that you can also convert your word document to a .mobi file by downloading mobipocket creator (www.mobipocket.com). After downloading the software, go into you word document and create a header at the beginning of every chapter. You can do this by placing your cursor at the beginning of each chapter heading then clicking on the Heading1 tab on the home page. This will separate each chapter in your ebook and also give your readers the ability to click on the chapter heading (i.e. chapter 3) and go directly to it. After doing this, you also need to download Amazon's previewer software which will give you the ability to preview your ebook to see if it's done to your satisfaction before downloading it to kindle or another ebook reading device.

How Many Copies Should You Start With?

When you decide to do a print version of your book, either before or after your ebook version, it is important to decide how many copies you want to have printed. I know you're going to sell a million of them, but since you're just starting out on this venture, I suggest you start out by only printing somewhere between 50-100 copies. That's just to test the waters and see what kind of response you'll get from the public. Plus, chances are you may still have a few errors in these first copies and you don't want to print a large amount with those errors in them. Printing a small quantity will give you an opportunity to correct any errors you may discover before going all out with a large order. After you place your order, make sure you store your books in a well ventilated area. While a garage or basement may seem like a good idea, they may not work unless they're well ventilated.

Chapter Summary

1) There are other alternatives to publishing besides traditional

2) POD is a viable option

3) Vanity and Subsidy publishing is risky and uncertain

4) Self-publishing places you in total control

5) Choose your printing company wisely

6) Take advantage of publishing with Amazon, Create Space, KDP, etc.

7) Print 50-100 copies to test the waters and correct unseen errors

Chapter Six

__Things Your Book Will Need__

I'm writing a book. I've got the page numbers done.
— *Stephen Wright*

Before you send your book off to the printer there are a few more details you need to take care of. One, is to make sure it's copyrighted. A copyright is what recognizes you as the original owner of your work and occurs automatically under common law as soon as you create your work. Many first time authors worry about someone stealing their material and calling it their own. A copyright protects you against this.

There are two ways you can obtain a copyright. One way (and the one I suggest) is to go online to the Library of Congress website (www.loc.gov). While there, click on eCO and file your copyright electronically. The cost is only $35 and your book will be officially copyrighted. Copyrights last the life of the author plus 70 years, so your work will be protected long after you're gone.

Another way to copyright your material is by using a method that's affectionately called "The Poor Man's Copyright." After you've completed writing your book, make a copy of it and mail it to yourself. When it comes back to you, don't open it. Keep it in a safe place so you'll know where it is in case you need it. In the event you ever have to use it (and I hope you never do), your sealed, stamped and postmarked envelope can be used as evidence in a court of law. Although it's not an official copyright like the one from the Library of Congress, it is admissible. I don't mean to alarm you with all this legal talk because the fact of the matter is if you're concerned about a publisher stealing your work, there's no need to be. They're not out to steal your idea and trust me, chances are they've already seen something similar to your work anyway. Despite what you might think, your work is not unique and not worth the hassle a publisher would have to go through in court. Besides, they're in the business of publishing books, not stealing them.

Now when it comes to you infringing on someone else's copyrighted material that's a different story. Unless you're only using a short excerpt of someone else's information from a book they wrote, you may have to get permission from the author or the publisher. You can use copyrighted material for research or teaching, but you can't sell it or call it your own. When using someone else's material, you must always indicate who they are and where you got the material. For example, the information I just gave you came from Dan Poynter's book, *Books: Tips, Stories and Advice on Writing, Publishing and Promoting,* and also from Loriann Hoff Oberlin's, *Writing for Quick Cash.* See how easy that was. This is not only the legal way to do business, it is the ethical way to do business, as well.

There's one thing that can't be copyrighted, that is a title. There are simply too many of them to keep track of. Copyright protects text not titles. Also facts and ideas cannot be copyrighted either. Most non-fiction books are written from research of other authors' work. If you see something you'd like to use, it's perfectly legal to use something from someone else's material, as long as it's not word-for-word. It has been said that if you use something from one author it's plagiarism, but if you use the same material from two or more authors, then it's called research.

Pricing

Like any product your book has to have a price. So how do you determine what the price of your book should be? Well to you I'm sure it's worth a million dollars, but let's be realistic. Although you think it's worth a mint, you know you won't be able to sell it for that much.

It's been reported that 26% of people who shop for books make their decision based on price. It is for that reason that you need to give careful consideration to the price of your book. You don't want to price it too high where no one will buy it, but you don't want to price it too low keeping you from making a profit either. That's why you have to do all you can to keep your printing and other costs as low as possible. The more you have to pay for these things the more you'll have to charge for your book to make a profit.

If you want to know how to price your book, it may be a good idea to go to a local bookstore and take a look at books that are similar to yours. Notice their size, material and page count. This should give you a general idea of what you should price yours for.

Another factor to consider in the pricing of your book is that of distributorship. A distributor will serve as a conduit between you and your customers. While most of your profit will be made by selling your books directly to customers face to face (where you'll collect 100% of the profits), you still need to establish some sort of distributorship. One of the best distributors to use is Amazon.com. Of course they'll charge you for their services, but that's okay because Amazon will give more people an opportunity to see your book than you can get on your own. (I'll talk more about this later in the promotion section.)

Sometimes authors will start out by pricing their books on Amazon.com as low as 99 cents in order to sell a lot of copies, and then raise the price later. Amazon charges a 30% commission on books priced between $2.99 and $9.99, and 65% on books priced higher or lower. Again this is why you need to choose your printing company wisely and shop around for the best deal. You'll need to deduct the price you pay per book printed to figure out your profit. Most distributors will charge between 30-65% to sell your book. While this may seem like a lot, compare that to the 75-90% a traditional publisher takes. That's why so many authors are choosing to go the self-publishing route where they can collect 100% of the profit for themselves. Of course it takes more time and effort to do it, but if done properly, it will be well worth it. Some authors choose to price their books between five to eight times their printing costs. Again, that's why it's so important to look at other books and see what their prices are before you make your final decision

Int'l Standard Book Number (ISBN)

An International Standard Book Number or ISBN is something that every book must have. It's a worldwide 13-digit identification system. Think of it as your book's fingerprint or social security number. ISBN's can be obtained individually for as little as $55 and for as much as $129. However, if you plan to write several books, you may want to purchase them as a group where you can order as many as 10 at a time. One place you can do this is www.bowkerlink.com. If you decide to create a different version of the same book (i.e. hard and soft cover), you will need different ISBN's for each version.

Barcode

Like any other product sold, a book needs to have a barcode. How else will a retailer be able to keep track of its sales or know what the price is when a customer brings it to the register? The barcode in addition to the ISBN, is used to identify the author, publisher, title and the version of your book that is being printed. In most cases, bookstores will not accept your book without it. The barcode should be placed in the lower right or left corner on the back cover and should include the price of your book as well as the ISBN. The printing company you choose should be able to get this for you, or you can obtain one yourself fairly inexpensively by visiting www.barcode-us.com. Before you order your barcode, you should already have decided what the price of your book will be and obtained an ISBN.

LCCN or PCN (optional)

Another item your book can include is something called a Library of Congress Control Number (LCCN) or Preassigned Control Number (PCN) if it is assigned prior to the publication of your book. Just as you can do with your copyright, you can apply for this number through the copyright office (www.loc.gov). This number is different from an ISBN because unlike the ISBN, you don't have to assign a new one for each edition. It is assigned to the work itself regardless of how many versions of the same book you have printed. The number is usually placed on the copyright page. Once you're assigned a number, it will be placed in a catalog that libraries use to find new books. You can also submit your book to a company called Follett Library Resources (www.flr.follett.com). If your book is accepted, they will send you a purchase order every month from libraries as they order your book. They will also place your book in their catalog where it can be purchased by every school librarian in the country.

CIP (optional)

The final thing you can place in your book is a Catalog in Publication (CIP). This is a separate Library of Congress service that supplies you with an additional catalog number and can be printed on the copyright page of your book. This number is used to help libraries shelve your book in the right category. After you've included the crucial components discussed in this chapter, your book will be ready to present to the general public.

Chapter Summary

1) There are two ways to obtain a copyright

2) The "Poor Man's Copyright" is not official but it is legal

3) Titles, facts and ideas cannot be copyrighted

4) Give careful consideration to the pricing of your book

5) All books need an ISBN and Barcode

6) Always give credit when using other people's material

7) You must assign a different ISBN to each edition of your book (hardcover and soft cover)

Section 3
How to Promote Your Book

Chapter Seven
Marketing and Promotion

Marketing is too important to be left to the marketing department.

— David Packard

Okay. So you've taken all the necessary steps to write and print your book, it is now time to do the most important thing, which is to market and promote it. Why is it the most important? Because it is the way you'll be able to let people know about you and your book. And let's face it, if people don't know you, they don't know you. And if they don't know about you or your book, how are they going to buy it? After all, that is why you're in the game isn't it? To make sales. That's the bottom line. That's why publishers do what they do. At the end of the day they're a business and they're in the business of selling books and so are you. So start thinking and acting like a business owner who's in the business of publishing and selling books. And how will you sell them? Well by promoting them, of course. Even if your book is published by a publishing company, it will still be up to you to sell them. What a lot of authors don't realize is that it's the publishing company's job to get your book on the shelves of bookstores and other outlets, but it is your job to let people know about it.

Ralph Waldorf Emerson said, "A funny thing happens without promotion…nothing." Truer words have never been spoken. Having said that, there are many methods you can use to market and promote your book. I will discuss a few of them in this chapter.

Word of Mouth

In this day and age of modern technology such as social media, text messages, and email, it seems to be more and more rare to see people talking face to face. However, despite the technological advantages these mediums afford you (and there are many), nothing beats talking to someone personally. You should tell everyone you come into contact with (at least those who come within three feet of you) about your book. Start thinking of yourself as an author and start calling yourself one. You have to take yourself seriously. If you don't, no one else will. Don't be afraid to toot your own horn because no one else is going to do it for you. Self promotion is the best promotion. You do it every day anyway, from the way you carry yourself, the way you dress, the way you talk, even the way you walk. Some people may feel awkward doing their own self-promotion because of their shyness. If this is you, get over it. Self-promotion is a must. There's nothing better than word of mouth, and the best word of mouth is yours.

Know Your Market

Before you can promote your book you first need to know who you want to promote it to. This is called your market. Your market is your target audience and you have to know who, what or where they are before you can do anything. That is, if you hope to be successful. Think about it. Would you go to a gardening convention to try to make sales if you've written a book about football? No you wouldn't. Why not? Because that's not where your market or your target audience is. You've got to figure out where to best utilize your time and energy. You may not get it figured out the first time. That's why you have to evaluate your efforts and strategies. Another self-publishing expert, Brian Jud[6], says that when it comes to marketing, everyone needs to have a P.I.E. strategy. The **P** stands for Plan. Before you get started you must plan your marketing strategy. The **I** is for Implement. After you've planned your strategy, now it's time to implement it. In other words, now it's time to put your plan into action. Then comes the **E**. It stands for Evaluate. After you've planned your strategy and implemented it, now you must evaluate it to figure out what worked and what didn't, so you can do it better the next time. Using this strategy and knowing where your target audience is are two vital keys to your success.

This same strategy is true when it comes to placing your book in bookstores, especially if you've written a specialty book. For example, if your book deals with surfing, you may be able to obtain modest sales by reaching a few people in a regular bookstore. But, think how many more people you can reach and how many more sales you'll get from placing your book in a store that deals with surfing, such as a sporting goods store or better yet, a surf shop. See the difference? That's not to say that you shouldn't place your book in a regular bookstore, it's perfectly fine to do both. I'm just saying you need to go where you can get the most success for your efforts.

Create a Website

If you're going to call yourself an author, having a website is a must. Otherwise, other than through word of mouth, how else are readers going to hear about you and your book? Having a website will go a long way towards the success of the marketing and promotion of your book. Now when it comes to the design of your website there are some important factors to consider. Deciding what to name your website is just as important as the design of it. While most people rack their brains trying to come up with fancy names and catchy phrases for their site, you don't have to do that. Why? Because you can just name your website after yourself (i.e. www.yourname.com). Naming your website after yourself gives it an identity and establishes your footprint on the web. All you have to do is visit a site such as www.godaddy.com or any of the others that allow you to purchase a domain name and search for one. After you find out whether or not yours is available, go ahead and purchase the domain and let the designing begin. There are several sites you can visit such as www.wordpress.com that will help you easily design your website yourself, or you may decide to hire someone who specializes in designing websites to do it for you. Regardless of how you decide to do it, you must get it done because a website is one of the most popular ways people search for books these days. This makes having a website an important key to your success because whenever a potential reader does a Google search of your name, your website will more than likely be the first thing that appears.

Once you've created your website, you should visit it often (at least once every few weeks) to make sure everything is working and still looks like you want it to. Checking it often may help you decide to update or even delete some of your information. Place your contact information on every page. Also, be sure to include testimonials from people who have benefitted from purchasing your book. Having a website will not only give you national exposure, but it will increase your sales potential internationally, as well. That's why a website is a must have for anyone desiring to be a successful author.

Start a Blog

In addition to creating a website, you should also start your own blog. The word *blog* is short for *web log*. This is a great way to keep up with people who are interested in you, your book, or just what you have to say in general. You can start blogging about a variety of subjects, be it a chapter of your book or anything else you'd like to talk about. You may even want to visit other people's blogs that are similar to yours and start writing comments on them. You'll be amazed at how many people share your common interests and are willing to put their two cents in. Use their opinions to get new ideas for your book or just to get their names on a mailing list. You can use this mailing list to keep your readers up to date on what's going on with you, in the industry or any new material you may have coming out soon. To get your mailing list started, create a sign-up form and place it on every page of your website or blog.

Create a Press Kit

Another good piece of information an author can use for promotion is what's called a press or media kit. It's an important packet of information that tells the public about you, the services you provide (if any), your book, and all your contact information. While most people will go to your website to find this information, from time to time it may be necessary to provide a hardcopy version of it. Distribute it at conferences and other events, or mail it to potential customers. It is also good to have a press kit available to pitch your work to TV and radio hosts before scheduling a potential interview.

So what items should you include in your press/media kit? In his book, *Before You Publish Your*

Book: 5 Essentials Every Author Must Know About Self-Publishing, my friend and mentor Hasani Pettiford[7], gives a very detailed list. He says no press/media kit would be complete without the following items:

1) **A Basic Bio:** This should be a 3-4 paragraph description about you and what makes you unique. It should also include a description of your current product and any media exposure you've acquired as well as your contact information.

2) **Testimonials:** While your bio is you bragging on yourself, a testimonial is others bragging on you.

3) **An Author's Photograph:** This should be a professional headshot of yourself.

4) **Book Info:** This should include the full title, ISBN, your name, publisher's name and date published. You may also include an order form.

5) **A Postcard:** This should have a picture of the cover of your book on one side and a brief description of the book on the other.

6) **A Book Excerpt:** This is a brief sample of your book you can give in order to whet the potential customer's appetite.

7) **Reviews:** If your book has been reviewed, include a copy of them and state who did them. Of course you only want to include the good ones.

You may or may not decide to use all of these suggestions, and of course there may be other things you may want to add to your press/media kit as well. Regardless of what you decide to use, be sure to include only up to date and current information.

Offer Discounts and Freebies

Although I'm sure you'd like to, you have to realize that you can't sell all your books, at least not at full price anyway. By that, I mean you're going to have to offer discounts on some of them and even give some of them away. You can discount them to wholesalers and distributors who will charge anywhere between 30-65%. This may sound like a lot, but keep in mind that they'll be able to get your book into places you may not be able to get it into on your own. You can also offer to sell your book in local bookstores which will normally cost you about 40% of your profits. Again this may sound like a lot, but keep in mind you're trying to gain as much exposure as possible, and it will cost you.

Another strategy you can use when it comes to gaining more exposure for your book is to give some of them away. While this may not seem like a good idea right now, sometimes it can really pay off. Of course you should only give them to people you feel can help you sell more, but from time to time there may be a few exceptions. I remember one occasion when I was first starting out with my books. I was taking care of some business at a local post office when I noticed a young lady there with her son. Since I write children's books, I felt the need to give her one and autographed it with her son's name in it. She was very appreciative. A few days later, I got a call from one of the local TV stations where she worked asking if I'd like to make an appearance on their morning show to talk about my book. I was so elated! That one act of kindness brought me more exposure than I ever could've imagined. That's the beauty of this business. You just never know who you might help, or who might be able to help you.

Like I mentioned earlier, some authors like to offer free downloads of their books on Amazon. This is another great way to gain much needed exposure. It's also a nice way to increase your chances of getting your book placed on a bestseller list, because believe it or not, these free downloads count as sales. However, I expect this to change soon if it hasn't already. Some authors refuse to offer free books because they feel it's unfair to offer a free download after others have already paid for copies of their book. The goal however for authors who do offer this is that hopefully people will order the free book and like it so much that they'll be willing to come back and purchase more, even after the free offer has expired. They may even ask their friends to do the same.

Another way to gain exposure through free giveaways is by donating a few copies to a charitable organization. You may even want to give free copies to people you know who work in the area you're trying to target (i.e. teachers at schools). You can also offer discounts to people who agree to pre-order copies of your book.

Radio and Television Interviews

When it comes to promotion there's no better outlet to use than radio and television. Setting up interviews on radio and TV stations are a great way to reach the masses. Unless you're a celebrity or someone with great name recognition, it can sometimes be difficult. However it is not impossible, especially on a local level. Most local radio and TV stations are always looking for local talent to spotlight on their shows, especially authors since most people view them as experts. People will tune in to listen to someone who they think has something interesting to say.

So how do you get the attention of radio and TV stations? You can start by contacting them by phone or email and sending them a copy of your press/media kit we discussed earlier. Find out who the producer of your local morning show is. Don't be afraid to call. They can only tell you yes or no; if you don't ask, you've already taken no for an answer. The best time to do this is when you have an upcoming book signing or seminar scheduled at a bookstore or library. If you will be attending another event where people can meet you and have an opportunity to purchase a copy of your book that would be another great time to contact your local media to set up an interview.

For many people, being on the radio or TV, even on a local level, can be quite nerve racking. The thought of thousands of people listening to your every word can be daunting. So continuously practice and brush up on your interviewing skills. You don't want to sound nervous or inarticulate when being interviewed. You want the listening audience to hear and see you as professional and believable, and as knowledgeable about your subject as possible. Before soliciting an interview, I suggest you practice with someone you feel comfortable with. Create your own questions and conduct a mock interview. During the interview, don't think of it as such, but think of it as two friends just having a casual conversation. If you view it this way, even during a live broadcast, you should be fine. Try not to think about the hundreds, thousands or maybe even millions who may be watching or listening to you. Don't concentrate on the cameras or microphones. Only concentrate on the host or interviewer. Of course all of this is easier said than done, but that's why you have to practice. And while practice won't make you perfect, it will go a long way towards making you feel more comfortable during an interview.

After you've scheduled an interview, again you can prepare your own questions for the host/interviewer. They may or may not have had time to read your book prior to your appearance, so they may appreciate this gesture. However, even if you have your own questions arranged for the interviewer, be prepared for them to deviate from the subject from time to time depending on the flow of the conversation and their own interest in your topic.

Another thing you can do to prepare yourself for an interview is to watch and listen to other people as they are being interviewed. Notice their mannerisms, their posture, and how well they answer each question. Also notice their enthusiasm. Enthusiasm sells. If you're not excited about your book, don't expect anyone else to be. Let your enthusiasm show during your interview be it on radio or on television. Remember you're there to promote your book, and you can't promote or sell anything without enthusiasm. I'm not saying you have to be overly dramatic, but you do need to be excited and proud of the fact that you've completed your book and you want to make sure everyone knows it. Zig Ziglar said, "For every sale you miss because you're too enthusiastic, you'll miss a hundred because you're not enthusiastic enough."

While showing enthusiasm is one thing you want to do during your interview, one thing you definitely do not want to do is over talk the host. Make sure you keep your answers to their questions short and to the point. I'm not saying you have to make them as simple as yes or no, but you don't want to drag out any of your answers by talking too long. Try not to make your answers longer than a minute or two. Again just be yourself and think of it as a normal conversation. When the interview is over, be sure to thank the host for allowing you to come on their show and talk about your book. Being a gracious guest will hopefully lead to more invitations for you to come back on their show in the future.

Host Your Own Radio Show

If you're not too keen on the idea of being a host on someone else's radio show to promote your book, then why not try your hand at hosting one of your own. Like so many other things these days, you can do it on the Internet. Log on to a site called Blog Talk Radio at www.blogtalkradio.com (you can also do a google search for others) and for a nominal fee and in some cases even free, you can host your own show. When registering you can choose the day and timeslot you'd like. You can also choose the title of your show and how long you want to be on the air (30 minutes, an hour, etc.). Also while registering, you'll be allowed to place certain buzz words or catch phrases pertaining to your book or show on your site so people can easily find you while surfing the web. After registering, you will be able to host your own show from the comfort of your home by using your home or cell phone. You will also be issued a web browser so you can chat live with your listeners, as well as a special phone number for your guests to call for the interview and your listeners to call to make comments or ask questions. Each broadcast is archived so you can go back and listen to it later. You can also upload it to facebook or other social media.

Have Your Book Reviewed

Few things will give your book credibility like a book review. If you're writing nonfiction it's normally for informational purposes, and chances are you've had to do a lot of research. After you've completed your book, Dan Poynter suggests sending chapters to experts who specialize in whatever each particular chapter is about. Of course you'd like to get a good review, but even if you don't, that's no reason to fret because even a bad review is better than no review at all. Besides, this will give you more exposure and it's cheaper than trying to buy advertisement.

Some reviewers will give you a negative review just to get a rise out of you or a potential reader. Don't take it personal. Some people may not buy your book because of a negative review. But, there are some who may buy it just to see what all the fuss is about, or they have some interest in what you have to say.

Believe it or not, some authors actually pay to have their books reviewed thinking it will garner positive results and boost their book sales. I don't think you should do this. Why pay to get someone's opinion? Don't you think it would be biased? If your book is good enough, you should get a positive review anyway without having to pay for it. To find out how to have your book reviewed, go online and check out blogs related to your specific genre and see if they offer them. Amazon will also allow you to offer your book on its site for free and request reviews. But, keep in mind, you're not selling the book, you're only putting it out there to gain reviews. As I mentioned earlier, going the self-published, POD, or vanity route will make it more difficult to get a review, but it's not impossible.

Attend Conferences

At the beginning of this chapter I mentioned the importance of knowing your market or target audience and how to reach them. One of the best ways to do that is to attend conferences that are put on by certain groups or organizations. This is how you gain exposure and begin creating a name for yourself. For example, most of the books I've written have been for children and I've sold thousands of them. I've sold so many by attending conferences, and not just any conferences. Remember earlier, I used the example of writing a book about football and how it wouldn't do you any good to try to sell it at a gardening convention? That's because that wouldn't be the right market. The same is true of children's books. Because of that, most of the exposure I get for my books comes from attending conferences that are dedicated to educators such as teachers, principals, school counselors and media specialists. I can't tell you how many I've attended over the years. Some have been profitable, while others have felt like a total waste of time. However I had to go to them if I wanted to be successful in this business, and I still attend them whenever I can. My wife, Sharmon, always says, "You have to kiss a lot of frogs before you get to your prince." And believe me, I've kissed a lot of frogs in my career. But, it's been well worth it. I always leave home never knowing whether I'm going to sell five books or 500 books at a conference, but I know I won't sell any if I stay home.

While at the conferences, I relish the opportunity of meeting the educators I mentioned earlier in hopes of getting an invitation to their school and doing a presentation for the kids with my books. Whenever I can secure an invitation to the school, I feel like I've hit the jackpot. My mission has been accomplished because once I get there I can sell even more books to the parents of their students. And on top of that, they'll also pay me a nice honorarium for visiting their school. See how this works? That's why it pays to know your market.

Speaking of knowing your market, sometimes you may not have to attend a conference, convention or a seminar, as long as you know what your market is. I always like to tell the story of how I attended a PTA meeting on a Tuesday night at a particular school and set up a booth. While there I think I only sold about three or four books. I'm not going to lie and tell you that part of me wasn't disappointed, at least until Friday of that same week, that is. That's when I received a call from the principal of that school who informed me that she wanted to purchase 500 of my books! She said she wanted every student in her school to have at least one of my books. I couldn't believe it. I almost dropped the phone! I felt like I'd struck gold.

When you attend conferences, there are several things you must do in order to make your trip worthwhile. First, research the conference. Find out the cost to reserve a booth and the deadline for registration. How far will you have to travel? How many days will you be there? Will you need to make hotel reservations? Will all of this fit into your budget? Visit the organization's website and find out how many attendees they had at their conference the previous year and if they expect about the same or more this year. Ask yourself, *If I can sell to 1% of attendees, will it be profitable?* You may even consider sharing a booth with another author to split the costs.

While at the conference, make sure you put your best foot forward by being well groomed and dressed in either business or business casual attire. Don't spend too much time sitting behind your table. Instead, spend most of your time standing in front of it, greeting all passersby with a smile, a firm handshake and inviting them to come over and take a look at what you have. Always be polite to everyone who stops by whether they purchase a copy of your book or not.

In addition to the factors I just mentioned, here are some other things you need to do before, during and after the conference:

- Plan your display, print and marketing materials (pens, brochures, bookmarks, etc.).

- Try to get a booth where the most traffic is.

- Decide whether you want to be near or away from your competitors.

- Create a banner. It doesn't have to be flashy but it does need to get people's attention.

- Make an overall impression by making sure your booth display is neat and orderly.

- Place a clear bowl with raffle tickets or some other sort of give away on your table.

- Have a sign-in sheet to get contact information to add to your mailing list.

- Send thank you e-mails or cards after the event.

- Take pictures of people at your display and send it to them.

- Evaluate your day. What worked? What didn't work? What can you do differently? Decide whether you'd like to attend next year.

Networking

The last thing I want to mention in this chapter pertaining to marketing and promotion is the importance of networking. Networking is defined as communicating with and within a particular group. I think of it as working with like minded people to achieve a certain goal. You have to create your own circle of influence or affiliates (people who can talk about or even sell your book for you). Realize that you can't do it all. Remember, I said a couple times earlier that one of my favorite sayings is, "It takes teamwork to make the dream work." Think of how many people you know and how many people know you. In other words, think of how many people you know who may be able to help you get to where you're trying to go. This may be another good reason to attend conferences. The networking opportunities are priceless, and the more you attend, the more opportunities you'll have. You may find people there who can give you all sorts of helpful information, and who knows, you may be able to help them as well. Use all the information and new friendships you gain to build your platform.

Another great way to network is to find online forums pertaining to your book's subject and join in on the discussions. Your book may be the answer to someone's problem. Brian Jud says every book should have a **PAR** statement. PAR is an acronym for **P**roblem, **A**ction and **R**esult. In other words, your book should address a certain problem and tell people what particular action or actions to take in order to achieve their desired result.

In addition to writing comments on online forums to bolster your networking and promotional opportunities, you can also go on social networking websites or other people's blogs to gain even more exposure. And last, but certainly not least, you can offer to speak for free to any organization you feel may be interested in your book. (I'll talk more about this in the next chapter.)

More Ways to Market and Promote

My friend and fellow author, Dwain Boswell[8] suggests adding a QR code to your business card or flyer to drum up more business. A quick scan of your QR code allows people to use their cell phone to be linked directly to your website. There are several other ways to market and promote your book in addition to the suggestions I have previously mentioned in this chapter. Some of them are:

- Send out emails to all of your friends and relatives announcing the release of your book.

- Take advantage of social media by creating your own page, starting or joining a group on Facebook, Twitter, Linkedin, etc.

- Contact newspapers and other publications that offer reviews, and ask if one can be done on your book.

- Create pens, bookmarks, postcards or other paraphernalia with the title or cover of your book on them and give them away.

These are just a few ideas you may want to employ along your journey to becoming a successful author. I'm sure there are others you may think of as well, like hosting your own book signing or seminar. In my opinion, a book signing may not be a good idea unless you're an established personality, or unless you do one at a bookstore that specializes in your book's subject. Why do I say this? Because most of the time people will only come to a book signing if they know you. This means that most of the people who come may only be your friends and family. Furthermore, a book signing is all about you and your book and we live in a society where most people live by the WIIFM philosophy, i.e. "What's In It For Me?" That's why

I think rather than hosting a book signing you should host a seminar, or combine the two together. That way, at least people will feel like they're getting something out of the deal, à la your expertise, and then they'll probably be more apt to purchase autographed copies of your book. Whatever method you decide to use, the bottom line is you want to make sure that you take full advantage of every opportunity to reach as many people as possible to let them know about you and your book.

Chapter Summary

1) The best word of mouth is yours

2) Know your market

3) Be sure to create a website

4) Be sure to create a press kit

5) Start a blog

6) Brush up on your interviewing skills

7) Attend conferences, conventions and seminars

Chapter Eight

The Business of Being an Author

I love being a writer. What I can't stand is the paperwork.

Peter de Vries

As I mentioned earlier, you need to develop a business mindset and start thinking of yourself as a business owner because now that you're an author, you're in the business of publishing and selling books. You've got to take yourself seriously. If you don't, no one else will. Writing your book is a creative act, but selling it is a business. Having your own publishing business may add to your credibility as an author, not to mention the tax benefits that come along with it. Some people are more creative than business minded, while others are more business minded than creative. You may be one or the other, or you may be both. If you are both, that's great. This goes back to your marketing we discussed earlier. Marketing people don't have to be authors, but to be a successful author you have to be a marketer.

Start Your Own Publishing Business

Now that you're starting your own business you need to develop a mission statement that describes your business and what it hopes to accomplish. In order to run a business you must be a self starter, self motivated and self disciplined. You've got to know your strengths and weaknesses, have will power, and be a risk taker. You also need to set short and long term goals for your business like selling a specific number of books within a certain amount of time. While doing all this, you need to avoid the common mistakes that a lot of business owners make like lack of research, inefficient marketing and poor management. Be sure to create a budget and don't spend all your money on production. It's not how much you spend that's important but rather how you spend it.

So what should you call your publishing business? As with any business, you want the name to be easy to remember as well as recognizable. However, unlike your website, you do not want to name your publishing company after yourself. Doing that screams amateurism. Like any other business, you need to establish your own brand and your brand is you. By that I mean you need to establish a reputation of doing business not only productively and effectively, but also morally, ethically and professionally as well.

In many cases, your abilities as a business owner will need to outshine your talents as an author. You'll need to establish a business mindset and learn to adjust your schedule from the normal 9-to-5 most people are used to. After you've decided on a name for your publishing business, you should go to your local courthouse and obtain a business license. You should also register your business with the Internal Revenue Service (IRS). When you do this, you will be assigned an Employee Identification Number (EIN). This will allow you to take advantage of certain tax breaks such as writing off materials you use for your publishing business like the purchase of a new laptop, ink cartridges for your printer, the costs of having your book printed, or trips taken to writing conferences. You may even be allowed to write off a particular room in your home if you use it as an office. Check with your tax accountant to find out what is and what isn't allowable. Also, be sure to keep all receipts from travel and lodging. If you mail your books or other products, keep those receipts as well.

Open a Separate Checking Account

When you're done registering your business locally and with the IRS, you should open a new business account at a bank that's different from the one where you have your personal account. Make sure you open it as a DBA which stands for Doing Business As. This account will be attached to your EIN as opposed to your personal account which is attached to your social security number (SSN).

Payment Structure

When someone purchases your book, be it in person, at a conference, or via your website, what payment methods will you accept? Will you accept cash and checks only, or will you accept major credit and debit cards? Hopefully you'll be able to accept them all. Although accepting cash and checks are the traditional methods of receiving payments and require no effort on your part, receiving payments via credit or debit cards will require you to make a few adjustments. Registering your business bank account with companies like Pay Pal (www.paypal.com), Square Inc. (www.square.com) and others will make your transactions safe and easy online and via your smart phone. This will be especially helpful while selling your books at conferences like we discussed earlier, because a lot of people prefer to make purchases with credit or debit cards so they can have a paper trail as opposed to using cash or a check. Besides, you don't want to give them any excuse for not buying on the spot.

Create Audio CD's

Now that you've finished writing your book, you need to start thinking of creative ways to sell and promote it. One of the best ways in addition to creating an eBook like I mentioned earlier is to create your own CD's. Creating CD's is an easy and inexpensive way to generate more sales of your book. Think about it. Writing a book takes a lot of time and effort, but creating CD's only takes a fraction of the time and a lot less effort. You may spend days, weeks, months or even years writing your book, but you can record CD's in a studio or in the comfort of your own home in a matter of hours. Not to mention the fact that in a lot of cases, some people are willing to pay more for a book on CD that they can listen to in their home, office, or car than they are for a hard copy of a book because of the convenience. This could mean more profit for you in the long run. While I could have included this information in the previous chapter regarding marketing and promotion, I chose to include it in the business chapter because selling CD's along with the hard copy and eBook versions of your book is more than a marketing strategy, it's a business transaction.

Become a Public Speaker

In addition to creating CD's, another great way to market and sell your book is by becoming a public speaker. Now I know for some this is easier said than done because when it comes to phobias, public speaking is still at or near the top of most people's list. You may be one of these people. If you are, hopefully I can calm your fears a little bit. I've heard some people say that they would rather swim across a river of hungry crocodiles than speak in public. If this is you, there are several things I think you can do to combat your fear. One of which is to join a local Toastmasters Club. These groups offer a great way to overcome your fear of public speaking in a nonthreatening environment. This organization has helped thousands of people worldwide, including me, overcome the fear of public speaking and become better speakers.

The art of public speaking need not be as hard or as scary as most people think; especially for you as an author. Why? Because as an author you'll be speaking about something you know a lot about, your book. And, although you may still shudder at the thought of standing before an audience and speaking, you really shouldn't because since you'll be speaking on something you're knowledgeable about, you'll already have half the battle won. Besides, speaking engagements are a great way to gain more credibility and confidence as an author as well as sell your books and CD's. Not to mention the fact that you could achieve great publicity and be paid handsomely for it.

When you're first starting out as a public speaker, understand that not all of your speaking opportunities will be paid engagements. But not to worry, it won't always be this way. You can use these opportunities as practice for when you hit the big time. You should take advantage of every speaking opportunity that comes along no matter how small or insignificant it may seem. You may not always get paid to speak, but you'll probably at least be allowed to set up a table and sell your books and CD's afterwards, which is called "back of the room sales". In many cases, this may make up for not being paid to speak. If you don't know how to get speaking engagements, maybe you should join a local or national speakers bureau www.nsaspeaker.org.

Regardless of whether you're being paid to speak or not, it is important that you always put forth your best effort whether you're speaking to an audience of 50 people or 50,000. That's why you've got to practice as much as possible and make sure you know your material inside and out. In other words, you've got to expertise yourself. How do you do this? By doing research and by reading as many books as you can find on your desired subject. Some experts suggest reading at least 10. This will help keep you abreast of ever changing statistics, facts and figures.

So there you have it. All the tools and information you need to fulfill your dream of producing, publishing and promoting your very own book. I'm sure there are other tricks of the trade and more information you'll learn along the way. The main thing is now that you've satisfied your curiosity of what to do and how to do it, it's time to get to it and start writing. All it takes is a little time and effort on your part. So what do you say? Are you ready? If so I say go for it! I wish you much joy and happiness on your journey to becoming a successful author! I look forward to seeing your book in print real soon.

Chapter Summary

1) Start your own publishing business

2) Start calling and thinking of yourself as an author and business owner

3) Your abilities as a business owner may need to outshine your talent as a writer

4) Register with online companies like Pay Pal and Square Inc.

5) Open a separate bank account

6) Create your own CD's

7) Become a Public Speaker

Book Checklist

1) Decide what you want to write and how you want to write it

2) Start your research

3) Decide when to set aside time to write

4) Design your cover

5) Decide how you want to publish (Traditional or Self)

6) Develop a marketing and promotion strategy

7) Establish Your Business

About the Author

C. L. Threatt developed a love for writing at an early age after he was entered into a poetry reading contest by his 7th grade literature teacher. After this experience, he began reading and writing poetry as a hobby and eventually started turning his poetry into children's books. He has traveled to hundreds of schools and various other facilities to educate, entertain, and inspire thousands of children and adults of all ages. He has hosted several seminars and workshops where he has taught many people how to pursue their dream of becoming a published author. He is not only an author and poet, but also a husband, father and grandfather. He lives in Odenville, AL (just northeast of Birmingham). He has written books for young children, teens and adults, as well as a collection of inspirational poetry and has been featured as a guest on several radio and television programs, as well as in magazines and newspapers. He believes everyone has a story to tell and a book in them just waiting to come out. He has made it his own personal mission to help anyone who so desires.

Resources

1) Tracey E. Dils – Writer's Digest Books

2) Dan Poynter – www.parapublishing.com

3) Arlene Miller – www.bigwords101.com

4) Charles Ghigna – www.fathergoose.com

5) Loriann Hoff Oberlin – AMACON Books

6) Brian Jud – www.bookmarketingworks.com

7) Hasani Petiford – www.hasani.com

8) Dwain Boswell – www.iamworththeeffort.com

C. L. Threatt welcomes inquiries about speaking at meetings, conferences, events and to various groups. For more information contact him at:

Ahava Publishing, LLC
65 Twisted Oak Circle
Odenville, AL 35120
(205) 213-8472

www.cedricthreatt.com

www.ahavapublishing.org

CL3tt@windstream.net